D1740371

Coping with Retail Giants

COPING WITH RETAIL GIANTS
Gaining an Edge Over Discounters

A. Coskun Samli

COPING WITH RETAIL GIANTS
Copyright © A. Coskun Samli, 2015.

All rights reserved.

First published in 2015 by
PALGRAVE MACMILLAN®
in the United States—a division of St. Martin's Press LLC,
175 Fifth Avenue, New York, NY 10010.

Where this book is distributed in the UK, Europe and the rest of the world,
this is by Palgrave Macmillan, a division of Macmillan Publishers Limited,
registered in England, company number 785998, of Houndmills,
Basingstoke, Hampshire RG21 6XS.

Palgrave Macmillan is the global academic imprint of the above companies
and has companies and representatives throughout the world.

Palgrave® and Macmillan® are registered trademarks in the United States,
the United Kingdom, Europe and other countries.

ISBN: 978–1–137–47633–3

Library of Congress Cataloging-in-Publication Data

Samli, A. Coskun.
    Coping with retail giants : gaining an edge over discounters /
  A. Coskun Samli.
      pages cm
    Includes bibliographical references and index.
    ISBN 978–1–137–47633–3 (hardback)
      1. Stores, Retail—Management. 2. Retail trade—Management.
    3. Marketing—Management. 4. Small business—Management.
    5. Consumer behavior. 6. Discount houses (Retail trade) I. Title.

HF5429.S274 2015
658.8'7—dc23   2014041902

A catalogue record of the book is available from the British Library.

Design by Newgen Knowledge Works (P) Ltd., Chennai, India.

First edition: April 2015

10 9 8 7 6 5 4 3 2 1

This book is dedicated to smaller independent retailers who can make a major difference in our quality of life. It is also dedicated to the memory of Stan Hollander of Michigan State University. He was a great scholar and my mentor. He gave me my first start. I am indebted forever.

Contents

Exhibits

PREFACE

This book is for retailers who are entrepreneurial, independent, and creative, and above all, capable of critically analyzing and explaining what is happening in the market in terms of economic changes, consumer needs, and communication networks. They analyze these and many other varieties and connect these changes to their own business. Thus, this book addresses decision makers who make a genuine attempt to give more to their customers and hence try to survive the retail jungle. This book is not a "how to" book dealing with step-by-step recipes. Rather, it attempts to bring theory and practice together and, by doing so, give a boost to all retail practitioners. But, above all, the book addresses small and medium-sized retailers who have a difficult time surviving the pressures of gigantic discounters and chains. This book deals with small and medium-sized retailers and provides directions on how to be more entrepreneurial and proactive, as well as how to create your own competitive advantage.

Retailing is the moment of truth in the capitalistic market system because the results of all the economic activity and economic gains are delivered to the consumer through retailing. If the economic system is creating consumer value, retailing is the main deliverer of it. Manufacturer's efforts either pay off or are wasted at this level of delivery. In this sense, retailing is the firing line for most marketing plans and managerial decisions as well as for consumer attempts to satisfy their needs and improve their quality of life.

In my earlier books (Samli 1998, 2004) I pointed out that retailing, despite its role and importance in the market place, has been rather neglected in marketing- and management-related literatures. Although much more sophisticated knowledge has accumulated in the marketing and management fields, only a small and rather simplistic portions of the research finds its way to retailing theory and its decision-making areas. This is despite the fact that about 20 percent of working Americans are employed in the retailing sector. This sector has been neglected either deliberately or by default. The retailing sector employs many young people and gives them the first opportunity in their career. I believe retailing courses must make a major attempt to bring theory and practice together. All in retailing must take such courses to advance the teaching and performance of this important economic sector.

It is critical to see that retail practice is strengthened if the theory behind the practice is understood and practiced.

THE CHANGING ROLE OF RETAILING

Since my earlier retailing book (Samli 2004) the economies of European Union (EU) and the United States have not been performing up to par. In relatively poorer economic conditions, retailing may become a mover of the economic activity. Germany, for instance, in recent years to combat recession has created more retailing jobs by splitting 40 hours per week jobs maybe two 25 hours per week jobs. It is easy to create more jobs in retailing; they are not too costly and the new jobs could give a reasonable start in the recession-driven economy. One may say retailing is playing the role of a counter-recessionary force.

IS THERE A RETAILING REVOLUTION?

In a dynamic society such as ours, an economic sector such as retailing is bound to be a dynamic area as well. The question is just how dynamic is it. Since the previous book there has been much activity related to social media utilization and online retailing. In this sense the retailing sector is going through a revolution. This revolutionary activity is providing consumers more choice, better information, and different conditions regarding retail location and delivery. But, with the not very favorable economic conditions there will be more and more retail establishments owned and operated by well-educated people who have a considerable understanding of retail theory and how such theory can be applied to their own specific businesses. As the society advances economically, consumers, by definition, seek better values generated by the retailing sector. This is a very powerful stimulus that will accelerate the retail revolution. This revolution will be primarily carried out by entrepreneurial owner-managers in small and medium-size retailing.

This book is aimed at the ambitious and entrepreneurial group of people, who can certainly make a difference in generating consumer value in our society and be rewarded for their efforts in the form of profits. It is expected that this group will accelerate the retail revolution that is in the making. Certainly, it is hoped that this book will appeal to professional researchers and retailing practitioners to provide guidance in their thinking and in their practices. The book raises some very important research-related issues that are very pertinent to survival in the retail jungle. As it stands, the retail revolution in some ways is also creating a retail jungle in which survival is necessary, but difficult. As the reader progresses through the pages they will observe that this book dwells upon the reasoning generated by cross-germination of theory and practice. The emphasis here, therefore, is on a proactive and strategic orientation based on research, reasoning, theory, and application. Although the primary targets of this book are small and medium-sized retailers, almost all of the discussion presented in the book is applicable to all types of retailing.

Exhibit P.1 illustrates the general orientation of this book. As can be seen, retailing theory is connected to the existing retail realities prevailing in the marketplace (or places). That would give the creative retailer the power to determine what is needed. These activities would give the necessary ammunition to construct a retailing strategy. It is not only theory-based strategy to be constructed, but particularly planning the implementation of this strategy that would make survival in the jungle a possibility. The performance evaluation would indicate if the strategy and its implementation are working. The feedback would then indicate what may be needed for improvement.

Exhibit P.1 Retail Strategy Development

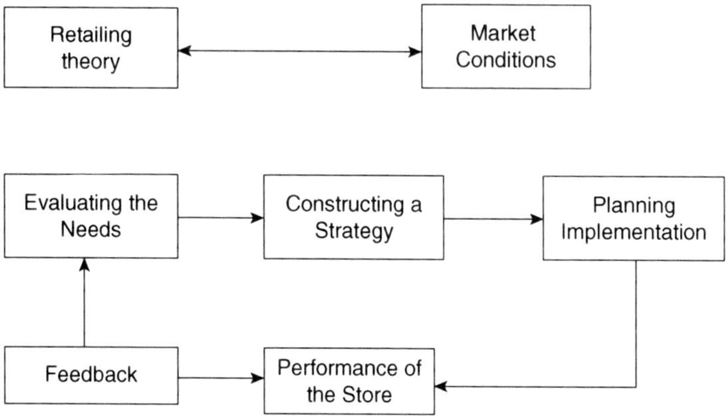

Source: Adapted and revised from Samli (2004).

Acknowledgments

My love for and activity in retailing started in Istanbul, Turkey when I was about 8 years old. I remember helping customers in my grandfather's shoe store by giving them mirrors. Later in my Uncle's shoe department in the family wholesale business, I remember putting signs "on sale" for some shoes. My interest in retailing continued all throughout my professional life. At Michigan State University, in addition to developing case studies, I worked with Stan Hollander who was considered at the time the most well-known retailing scholar. In my long career I worked with literally hundreds of small retailers. They helped me to develop knowledge and wisdom.

Certainly, I hope that my activities help them also. I am still teaching, researching, and consulting quite actively in retailing related areas. I still enjoy exchanging ideas with my students particularly in retailing.

Of course, having the opportunity working with many colleagues and exchanging ideas is still some pleasure despite of my 55 years of academic career.

Professor Adel El-Ansary of the University of North Florida has been a source of encouragement and important ideas. Professor Joseph Sirgy of Virginia Tech has been a friend, a coauthor, and a valuable colleague to discuss ideas.

My good friend Ed Mazze of the University of Rhode Island, over the years, discussed with me many issues related to retailing. Dr. James Littlefield of Virginia Tech, after many years, still is available to discuss problems related to retail marketing. Professor Ronald Adams of University of North Florida is available to interact with and to exchange ideas. I interact with him daily. Two younger colleagues at the University of North Florida, Dr. Saurabh Gupta and Dr. Youngtae Choi, have been very helpful to construct chapters 8 and 9.

Certainly Dr. Bruce Kavan of University of North Florida has been always willing to discuss my controversial ideas. My dean at the University Dr. Ajay Samant has been encouraging and supportive during the development of this book.

My student of earlier years and earlier research assistant, currently a very active retailing executive, Mehmet N. Ongan, is an important source of information and ideas. I hope to continue utilizing his wisdom in my research. My brother Osman Samli is always a phone call away. His knowledge of business has been very useful to formulate my orientation. My daughter Dr. Ayla Samli is a deep thinker and understands the societal issues well.

During the past year and a half I had three graduate assistants—Caitlin O'Keefe, David Alvarez, and Dimitri Ditombi; they contributed to my knowledge base. All have been always ready to explore issues for me.

Susan Watts, as usual, typed the whole manuscript; she is a magician being able to read my handwriting. She always does a great job. Bill Watts reads my manuscripts and makes invaluable comments to improve. I owe him a lot.

Finally, my eternal critique, my wife Bea Goldsmith must be acknowledged. She knows much about retailing but I prefer her skills as an outstanding chef.

To these and many other people who influenced my thinking and my knowledge base over the years, I extend my heartfelt gratitude. I hope that this book will mark a modest but noticeable contribution to the challenging world of small retailing. This certainly would be my repayment to the people who helped me. I would consider myself very fortunate and highly rewarded if many retailers read this book and benefit from it.

About This Book

This book as perhaps all books begins with an Introduction that identifies the importance and dynamic nature of retailing.

Chapter 1 discusses an important but a neglected topic of a number of important activities must take place before opening a store.

Chapter 2 introduces an important concept that is emphasized throughout this book, differential congruence. It means that as retailers we have to differentiate our operations in such a way that they will satisfy our customers' needs but we will not be similar to those who are competing with us.

Chapter 3 discusses different layers of retail competition and how each layer impacts our store.

Chapter 4 deals with the major trends in this very dynamic sector called retailing. If we don't understand the major trends that are impacting our business, we may not be able to survive and prosper.

Chapter 5 complements chapter 4 by presenting an evolutionary picture that applies to the retailing sector.

Chapter 6 explores how to capitalize on the existing potentials in the market. Certainly the key question here is "just what are the market potentials?" A few approaches are presented here to identify the opportunities that may exist in the identified target market of a retail establishment.

Chapter 7 takes on a very important but often neglected topic of how consumers behave in the retail market and what are implications of this behavior to the wellbeing of our store.

Chapter 8 complements chapter 7 by identifying retail strategies that may be used to satisfy the consumer needs in our market and generate consumer value.

Chapter 9 deals with developing, measuring, and managing the retail store's image. It must have a positive impact on its customers.

Chapter 10 explores the human element in retailing. In smaller independent retailing people, who work there, are the strength of the total operation. Providing good opportunities and treating well are critical to get good service from store's employees.

Chapter 11 points out that unless we learn to communicate with our market, we cannot possibly survive.

Chapter 12 explores just what are the features of the most appropriate merchandise mix.

Chapter 13 maintains that pricing is critical in retailing. Without a good price mix, the retailer stands no chance in the retail jungle.

Chapter 14 develops the newly emerging concept of retail logistics. It points out that we must understand when we are part of a larger system and when we are alone in dealing with our target market.

Chapter 15 posits that the final analysis is an ongoing process in a dynamic environment. Therefore, there must be regular control and evaluation so that we can learn to be better.

It is hoped that these 15 chapters could provide a strong orientation to surviving in the retail jungle. I hope that my 55 years of research and consulting experiences, hopefully, will make an impact.

INTRODUCTION

Any viable and proactive society must generate and distribute consumer value. This value is generated by the society's economic activity and distributed mainly by retailing. The consumer value that is generated by that society must be satisfactory for the whole society and must be delivered equitably and efficiently. Therein lies the challenge for the retailing sector. But, that sector is rather volatile and constantly experiences sharp turbulences. Many economic changes apply competitive pressures and consumer needs make it absolutely necessary that each and every retail establishment offer some value to the market. If the market does not appreciate what is being offered by the retailer it is the curtain for that retailer. This scenario repeats itself constantly in a dynamic economic system such as ours.

Walmart, the largest retailer in the world, at the writing of this book posted sales of 443 billions of dollars for 2012 in 27 countries by 11,000 stores, a remarkable increase since July 2, 1962. It employs 2.2 million workers. This progress indicates the golden era of discounting. It is not necessarily true that consumers worldwide have less money and as such frequent discount retail establishments. It is perhaps that consumers have become more informed and are able to exercise their preferences more often. But, for every Walmart store there are thousands of retailers who cannot be as low priced as Walmart. Yet, they have to survive, make a contribution to the consumers' well-being and survive, and, hopefully, prosper. But, as will be repeated a number of times in this book many of these retailers can be better than Walmart in terms of their customer services. These points are discussed throughout this book in some detail.

In the meantime, the largest retailer in the world for about 70 years, Sears, has been having a difficult time. In 2012 the company reported a loss of about $3.1 billion. This is, at least partially, because its target market which has been middle-class America has been shrinking. Sears customers moved down to lower-middle-class status. Another powerful retailer, Target, managed to appeal to this group with substantial impact. That chain emerged as an upscale discount department store chain. Its number of stores increased from 216 in 1984 to over 1,100 in 2000.

Another unusual example is Domino's Pizza which had scaled down its offering from a regular Italian restaurant to just take-out pizza. As a restaurant it did not do well; as a take-out pizza operation, it did very well. By it had nearly 2,000 plus units scattered throughout the United States. The annual sales volume for this company surpassed over $600 million. By 1990 the company had been experiencing a substantial increase in its competition. The company's sales volume had declined in the early 1990s. In 1994, the company diversified its services. Its expanded menu included salads, sandwiches, and chicken wings. Along with implementing a new and aggressive marketing strategy, its sales volume started to grow again. Despite two very powerful competitors, Pizza Hut and Dominos, it achieved a sales volume of 7.4 billion globally.

Publix supermarkets, an upscale chain with special emphasis on baked goods and deli departments, had been and is pursuing a relatively slow but deliberate growth strategy, primarily in better-than-average consumer income areas in Florida. While it operated 351 stores in 1988, in 2013 this number went up to 1,073 stores, generating a sales volume of $27.5 billion.

On the other end of the spectrum, Gillies, a small ice cream parlor in a university town in the Southeast, was doing very good business during the summer months, but the long winter months were not profitable enough to stay in business. The manager decided to offer a major change in the menu, particularly for the winter months. Gillies started offering a most unusual series of soups and sandwiches, along with interesting mugs, tee-shirts, and local artwork. Gillies turned out to be a place to spend some time with friends and became very successful.

These examples should illustrate the dynamic nature of the retailing sector and the importance of developing a proper marketing strategy. That strategy would either make or break the individual retailer. It must be kept in mind that there are millions of Gillies in the United States struggling for survival.

Surviving for small and medium-sized retailers in the shadow of the giants is not easy. It is like surviving in a jungle that has many overgrown and not so friendly creatures that could destroy us. However, as we function in that jungle, we learn a lot of things from these giants. If learning truly takes place, the knowledge received can be extremely beneficial for our survival. Perhaps the most alarming feature of the retailing sector can be observed in the small-scale retailing area. Hundreds of thousands of new establishments enter into the retailing arena and almost that many leave because of failure or bankruptcy. That makes the retailing sector almost like a jungle where survival requires a carefully constructed strategy regardless of whether they are Target or Joanny's Gifts. The small ones, however, are more vulnerable to economic conditions. In the retail jungle the rule may not be survival of the fittest, but survival of the fattest since the retail giants have enough resources to survive a recession or some other adversity in the market. Those many thousands of small and medium sized retailers that disappear most likely did not have a game plan or their respective strategies simply did not work out and either they were too naïve that they did not see the danger soon enough or they simply could not change their strategy in time.

It must be emphasized that unless the retailer thinks in terms of carefully constructed strategic planning and acts accordingly, the chances of survival followed by growth and prosperity are quite limited. The retail jungle is simply too difficult to survive in.

When retail organizations, both large and small, make a major shift from the old-fashioned orientation of merchandise management which means only sell, sell, sell to a strategic marketing orientation of creating and delivering consumer value, then the probability for success and survival increases. Thus, if we want to survive in the retail jungle, a properly constructed and implemented strategic plan must be the focal point of our thinking and our functioning. This book is a major effort in constructing retail strategy in its implementation, adjustment, and control. Particularly the small and medium-sized retailers whose survival in the retail jungle is extremely difficult must have a strategic orientation of planning their activities carefully rather than functioning in an unrealistic emotional manner.

All retailers must present a unique competitive advantage in the market. This competitive advantage is generated by the retailers' strategic posture. This will be a unique way on the part of the retailer to generate customer value that could lead to having a group of satisfied and loyal customers who like to shop at that retailer's place of business. The pursuit of competitive advantage is not necessarily a typical activity that is usually found in the average retail marketing situation. It is a skill that needs to be developed. The essence of this book is about developing that skill through strategic planning and implementation. Strategic retail marketing that will improve the chances of survival and perhaps prosperity in the retail jungle requires going beyond day-to-day activities, following simple "now to" approaches, or implementing so-called fail-safe recipes that do not even work.

This book presents a series of logical and research-based steps which would enable small and medium-sized retailers to become more viable and prosperous. Throughout the book, we discuss the conditions that will lead to better understanding of the necessary sequential steps and related necessary actions to be performed so that successful retail marketing strategy is in place and making a contribution to the existing quality of life.

First, it is important for the entrepreneurial retail decision makers to realize that one does not need to be "all things to all people." A small boutique, for instance, can do quite well with four or five hundred loyal customers who would spend about $2,500 annually for their wardrobe. Second, the entrepreneur must make sure that the presence and functions of the retail establishment is making a contribution to the well-being of its customers.

Visiting the Retail Jungle

As we visit the retail jungle we could easily state that "Retail Darwinism" is very much alive and kicking. There are a number of very powerful trends that are constantly reinforcing the unfriendliness of the retail jungle. If we were engaged in the general activity of starting an independent retail establishment or entering into the existing retailing arena in one of the multiple entry alternatives, it is crucial that we fully understand the implications of retail Darwinism on our business. Although it may still mean the survival of the fittest, at this point in time in our economy it is becoming survival of the fattest.

There are at least four key types of forces that are accelerating retail Darwinism and making the retailing sector truly a jungle for the small and medium-sized retailers. These four types of forces are: market-related forces, competition-related forces, consumer-related forces and technology-related forces (Exhibit I.1).

Market-Related Forces

The American economy is cyclical. At the writing of this book very slow progress in recuperating from the great recession is showing no inflation and no deflation. Of course when the economy sneezes, the retailing sector catches pneumonia. Hence, many small retailers do not survive. They are vulnerable to changes in the economy.

On the other hand, when the economy is experiencing a recession, an unusual development may take place, that is, costs and prices going down. That is deflation. It does not happen too often but when it does the retailer becomes puzzled since its inventory loses its value. Retail profits disappear and small profit margins become even smaller.

Exhibit I.1   Key Forces behind Retail Darwinism

Market-Related Forces
- Growth rate
- Inflation or deflation
- Value chain evolution

Competition-Related Forces
- Wal-Mart
- Supercenters
- Warehouse clubs

Consumer-Related Forces
- More sophisticated and better informed consumers
- Better communication
- Speedier reaction to consumer requirements
- High-quality, low-cost merchandise needs
- More and better service required
- Better consumer-focused assortments
- Ethnicity and personalized service

Technology-Related Forces
- Smart stores
- Scientific retailing
- Special media
- Big data

Source: Adapted and revised from Samli (2004).

Retail distribution channels during the past decade or so have been named value chains or supply chains. As the products initiated at the manufacturing level approach the retailer, advocates of supply chains maintain that value is added to these products because of proximity to the market, further adjusted forms, convenience for the consumer, and the like. As the supply-chain revolution becomes more and more of a reality, large retailer may benefit from them, and small and medium-sized retailers may not benefit from this arrangement because they are restricted by the rules established. The initiator of the supply chain could establish many rules that may hinder the actions of the small retailers.

Competition-Related Forces

In the past three decades or so there has been a remarkable movement on the part of discount giants. Walmart, Costco, Sam's, B.J.s, and others have emerged and mostly captured a big portion of retail sector. Thus, a tremendous competition for all types of traditional retailers has become a fact of life. As such, nontraditional retailers have been creating a new type of competition.

Consumer-Related Forces

Today's consumers are much more informed and sophisticated than their earlier counterparts. They also have a much wider choice of products and services, as well as much greater information and speedier service. Products they buy are of better quality and are reasonably priced. The retail assortments are much more to their liking. At the same time, there appear to be more ethnicity and personalization in the services the modern consumer is requiring.

Technology-Related Forces

Information technology and social media during the past decade or so has enabled consumers to demand certain products and services as pointed out above. On the other end of the spectrum, many retailers have adapted new advances in technology to improve their operations. Smart stores are becoming more involved in personalizing their customers and providing better services for them.

OBJECTIVES OF THIS BOOK

Given the hostile atmosphere surrounding the modern small and medium-sized retailers, this book emphasizes how they could increase their competitiveness and enhance their chances for survival and prosperity. At least five key orientations are emphasized for entrepreneurial retailers to succeed: (1) to use reason in retail decision making, (2) to bring theory and practice together, (3) to be able to construct retail strategies, (4) to develop skills to implement the strategy, and (5) to learn how to assess the effectiveness (see Exhibit I.2).

Although this book is written with small and medium-sized retailers in mind, most of the thinking and orientation could easily apply to larger retailers as well.

Reasoning behind Retail Decisions

Above all, this book emphasizes the fact that behind every retail decision and action there must be a solid reason. However, in real life not all reasons are based on factual information. Reasoning-based decisions must reflect knowledge, experience, and deduction. They would lead in the direction of making consistent, long-lasting, effective decisions that will create consumer value and generate profit. Retailing is not a "catch-all" activity displaying whimsical behavior. It is not a form of

Exhibit I.2 The General Orientation to Success

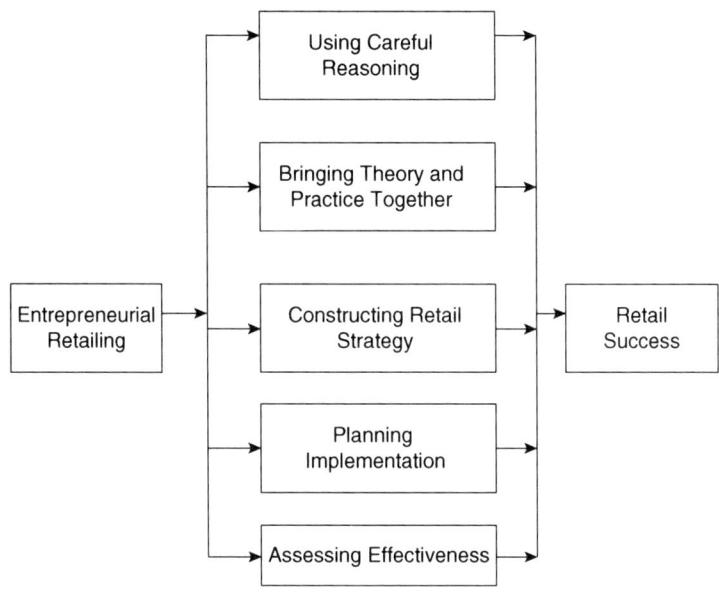

Source: Adapted and revised from Samli (2004).

gambling. Good retailing is based on understanding the consumer needs, identifying market forces that play a critical role and constantly changing and reasoning out the best possible solutions to generate maximum consumer value.

Bringing Theory and Practice Together

The reasoning I mentioned earlier cannot be effective if the retail establishment cannot incorporate its reasoning-based decisions with retail theory. Good reasoning stems from bringing the theory and practice together. Retail research literature combined with economic theory, and would provide a good foundation for effective decisions (Samli 2004). It is essential to realize that behind every good decision there is a theoretical stance.

Planning the Strategic Posture

All retailers, from the largest to the smallest, must have a game plan which we call strategy. Having a strategic plan implies not only possessing an effective game plan but also knowing how it may be implemented. After all, having a game plan that cannot be put to use is nothing but wishful thinking. Wishful thinking has no practical value. The modern retailer must be in a position to identify the strategic options and how they may be implemented. All of these need to be prioritized logically and reasonably.

Implementing the Strategy

In making a strategic decision the retailer must consider its implementability. There is a fine line between implementability and implementation. Whereas implementability signifies how a proposed strategy might be put to use, implementing that strategy is the action that will make or break the retailer. It would imply having concrete plans to make the strategic choice to work.

The implementation plan identifies and prioritizes the five retail mixes that are discussed throughout this book: (1) goods and services mix, (2) communication mix, (3) pricing mix, (4) human resource mix, and (5) logistics mix. These were discussed in chapter 1. The contents of these mixes and their relative importance are likely to vary from one type of retail store to another. However, the management's knowledge and decision-making capabilities play the most important role in enhancing survival and profitability of the retail establishment. Thus, every game plan is different, but some are not as good as others. This is what makes retailing a fine art and science since it includes profound logic with a personal artistic touch. This is where the theory and practice meet. The personal touch in an artistic manner is the entrepreneurship that is needed for every retail establishment. Here, being creative and proactive supported with knowledge and theory certainly pays.

Assessing Effectiveness

It is essential that we know the impact of our strategy. If we develop a strategic plan and decide how to implement it, but we do not have a way of determining if we are being effective or not, we are in a dangerous zone. Along with developing the strategy and planning its implementation, there must be plans to track down the effectiveness of this activity. The success or its lack thereof must be detected as early as possible. Knowing that the results of our actions are deviating from the planned results must be determined early and corrective action must follow immediately. Every retailer must have certain early indicators that can be used for this purpose.

The discussion presented here thus far implies the need for a very strong presence of entrepreneurship in successful retailing activity. Entrepreneurship, by definition, indicates presence of creativity, leadership, strong performance, and strong adaptability. Entrepreneurial activity displays a very strong sense of independence, which is important in all types of retailing activity. The five-step management activity identified in this book is the general orientation that needs to be used by the entrepreneurial retailers for success. Exhibit I.2 illustrates how the entrepreneurial orientation would lead to success. This exhibit presents the philosophical orientation of this book. All retailers must make decisions based on reasoning and theory. They must all develop strategic alternatives and must be proactive in implementing them. Finally, the results must always be quickly and accurately assessed.

SUMMARY

Retailing is a very dynamic sector. This makes it necessary for the retailer to go for choice and not chance. However, going for choice must be based on combining theory and practice. In doing so, the independent and creative touch of a retailer or entrepreneurship must always be present.

1

PREOPENING PREPARATIONS

Consider the two following stores. Store one looked for a low-rent place and went to an area which is off the beaten path; the store did not have a nice appearance; the owner manager assumed that customers would come to the store regardless; this did not happen and the store went bankrupt.

Store two looked at a number of location possibilities and finally located at a very active side of a mall. The owner manager planned the stores appearance, made many preopening announcements, and did not mind paying very high rent for a location that created heavy traffic. It became very successful.

This is rather an uncultivated area in retailing, planning and implementing preopening. But in this day of significant retail competition which is discussed in many sections of this book, having a plan of action before the retail establishment is opened can be rather important.

Whether it is an addition to a chain or an independent store, two broad areas needed to be considered: first what kind of information is needed to be communicated, and second how should it be communicated, that is the preopening promotional activity.

Exhibit 1.1 presents a basic list for general preopening promotional activity that must be considered. As it is reiterated throughout this book, the worse thing in a market system is being a well-kept secret. Without prepromotion the retailer becomes a well-kept secret. This certainly is a major consideration for a new retail establishment.

WHAT ARE OUR STRENGTHS?

Even though not confirmed or accepted by its customers, the prospective retail establishment must have certain features or certain functions in mind as its strengths. For an existing chain, there always is an image. The question is do we want the continuation of that particular image or do we want to modify it for local conditions is the

Exhibit 1.1   A Preliminary Checklist for Promotion

- What are our strengths?
- What do we promise to accomplish?
- Do we have an image to project?
- Do we have a proper checklist?
- Who do we communicate with?
- How do we communicate?
- How much are we likely to spend?

issue. On the other hand, if we are dealing with a new independent retailer we must realize that whatever we promise at that stage is likely to become what is going to be expected from us. That expectation is the beginning of the emergence of a prospective image. That image is the evidence of differential congruence.

WHAT DO WE PROMISE TO ACCOMPLISH

Although every retail entity has certain strengths, the location and the immediate community which may be called the primary market may have needs other than the strengths of the incoming retail establishment. If the local needs and strengths of the incoming retail establishment are completely different, for instance say the new retail establishment is a specialist on health foods but, the community really needs low-price foods, this becomes a total mismatch and it should not materialize.

DO WE HAVE AN IMAGE TO PROJECT?

If we are starting a new retail establishment, we have to develop an image that will differentiate that retail establishment from others. Here the image and perhaps a slogan must reflect that retail establishment and its own perceived vision by the market. "Just do it" or "save money live better" are well-known slogans supporting a proposed image.

But if we are dealing with a new addition to Nordstrom, which is a major upper-middle-class chain, it will be totally wrong to go against the Nordstrom image. It is necessary to implement the same image all Nordstrom units project.

DO WE HAVE A PROPER PREOPENING CHECKLIST?

If a retail establishment is in the process of being opened, the preopening promotion is so critical that we must have a complete checklist of whom and what is to be communicated.

Let us assume for instance that we are considering opening a gym in a small community of Maine. Before we prepare a checklist we must explore, for instance, was there a gym that discontinued its functions in the region? If there was one, is there a possibility to get their membership list similarly, are there a number of organizations with many workers, and are they interested if these workers exercised? Additionally, what are the local most effective mass media? Are there possibilities of local Chamber of Commerce or local administration that may sponsor us? Certainly depending upon the community and type of business, it is possible to have many other alternatives. After many alternatives having been considered, it becomes possible to construct a preopening activity checklist. Most of the items that should be considered are discussed below.

WHO DO WE COMMUNICATE WITH?

In all of the preopening considerations, it is necessary to consider the target market the proposed retail establishment is considering. Unless it is a giant discount store, a small independent retailer needs to be able to communicate with its target market. It is critical that the preopening activities are not wasted by communicating with everyone in the assumed trading area.

HOW DO WE COMMUNICATE?

This question needs to be answered by following the checklist mentioned above. That checklist provides the basics of preopening communications. Effort must be made to reach out to the prospective market.

HOW MUCH ARE WE LIKELY TO SPEND?

As discussed in different sections of this book, perhaps the most important consideration is not to have a specific budget at the beginning preopening communications activity. It is necessary to determine just what is going to be done and then how much all this will cost. Establishing a budget figure before all of the preopening activities are considered could be very limiting and quite inadequate.

PHYSICAL PREPARATION

In the final analysis, it is the physical facility that is going to make the total impact. It is, therefore, critical to plan the store in terms of what appeal it may project and if it can carry out the projected image.

Exhibit 1.2 Preopening Consideration of the Physical Facility

- The outside appearance
- Temporary signs
- Consistency with other retailers
- Internal layout
- Convenience versus attractiveness
- How much are we likely to spend

Whether or not the retail establishment fits into the other retail institutions surrounding in terms of appearance or must have much different appearance to attract attention needs to be decided at this point.

Exhibit 1.2 presents six very general areas that need to be considered before the retail establishment is opened for business.

The Outside Appearance

This is the first and probably the most important consideration. The store's physical appearance must be attractive to encourage consumers to explore. Being attractive also means ability to communicate with the prospective customers. Here, what the appearance physically conveys as a message and what additional physical messages must be added are very important questions and must be considered very carefully. Additionally, the store, although it may make a statement by its appearance, must also be somewhat consistent with other stores in the total shopping complex. If, for instance, the shopping complex is projecting a dynamic and youthful picture, the new proposed retail establishment should not project a somewhat static and, say, very conservative image.

Temporary Signs

Any starting retail establishment may have some signs such as "soon XYZ is coming here," or, "XYZ will be open for business at certain date," or some variation of such signs. Not only should they be attractive and readable, but also they must be very factual. If the proposed store did not open at the time the sign announced, it will create a major disbelief to anything the store will claim later.

Consistency with Other Retailers

As discussed in chapter 3 as a group, the retail stores project a synergistic image. In order to be a part of that synergistic power, the proposed retail store needs to be consistent not only with appearance, but also in terms of its offering. Again, if the total retailing complex addresses dynamic and youthful groups of consumers, the proposed new store needs to be at the same wavelength or needs to look at another location which may be more suitable for what it projects and what it promised to achieve.

Internal Layout

This is a critical preopening expenditure item. The proposed retail establishment must have an internal plan indicating how the merchandise is likely to be displayed and what type of customer traffic is likely to be expected. Again, based on the total image the store is expected to project, the internal décor must be consistent. The first expression and expected image of the internal appearance and convenience for customer shopping is likely to have a rather long-lasting positive or negative impact.

Convenience versus Attractiveness

For a shopper, convenience versus the attractiveness of the store's layout can be puzzling. Is there any way that these two extremely important concepts can be consistent with each other? In fact, they were consistent, meaning that the store layout is arranged in such a way that it is more convenient for customers to shop, but is also an attractive layout of the store's interior. This certainly could create a synergistic impact for the store and could make the shopping experience very attractive.

How Much Are We Likely to Spend

The answer is necessary as mentioned earlier. Establishing a budget figure in advance is not appropriate. It is extremely important that the proposed retail establishment be able to accomplish what it was set out to do.

Utilization of Social Media

Different types of social media are in the process of emerging. Some of these can be used for preopening information dissemination. Similarly, the proposed new retail establishment must have online offerings with pictures and attractive prices. But, particularly bringing the prospective customers to the physical facility and connecting with them individually are extremely important activities. Here, the new retail establishment may consider developing some entertainment and special prices.

The Psyche of the Entrepreneur

The owner/manager of the proposed retail store must believe in what is being offered to the market. The entrepreneur, above all else, may ask what the proposed store's primary emotional space is. In other words, to what extent this store will become a well-liked place to be shopped in. Then, the mental question may be raised as to how unique the place is. Is it the first in the market or is it similar to others? The owner/manager may further ask "am I offering performance benefits?" This may be followed with a question, "just who are my core customers?" Finally, two mental questions may be raised: first, am I offering a technically strong and emotionally engaging place and second, do I have certain plans for major future advancements?

Summary

This brief chapter deals with a very important, but not carefully culti-vated issue of preopening. It is extremely important that a proposed, new retail establishment must be properly promoted. That promo-tional effort must be supported by the physical entity. If there are not enough financial facilities, it should not be opened.

But, above everything else, the entrepreneur must have the proper attitude and psychological makeup so that what is being done here is the right thing.

2

RETAIL MARKETING STRATEGY DEVELOPMENT

A retail establishment must have certain features that distinguish it from others. Those features will enable consumers to identify it and be attracted to it. At the same time, these distinguishing features should dissuade consumers from patronizing other retail establishments for the same products or services. The unique and distinguishing characteristics of the particular store must be appealing to prospective customers. This means the unique characteristics of the retail establishment must be congruent with what its customers would like to buy. That is the winning strategy in retailing, which is coined "differential congruence" (Samli 2004).

THE THEORY OF DIFFERENTIAL CONGRUENCE

It is maintained here that if the congruence between the stores features and the customers' preferences synergistically becomes the unique features that clearly differentiate the store in question from others, then the store is optimizing its market opportunities. It is maintained throughout this book that small and medium-sized retailers are more able to accomplish differential congruence than the retail giants. This means the store, through its offerings and its personality, makes a distinct attribution to its customers' wellbeing. Such synergy improves quality of life for its customers, which simultaneously improves the store's probabilities for success.

The Legacy of Two Stores

In a small, southeastern town there are two upper-middle-class ladies apparel stores. Store one is located at one end of a busy mall, presenting simple and understated elegance. Store employees (who garner very attractive discounts for their own purchases) are well known for their social ties. The store is run like an almost ongoing party. The employees invite their friends to try new merchandise and socialize. The store owner/manager, who is well known in the community, will not allow a customer to leave the store unhappy. There is always a glass of wine, a home-baked cake, or exotic Russian tea available for consumption. This little store is extremely profitable because of its *differential congruence*. What it offers and what makes it unique are very well accepted features by its customers. This dynamic synergism is ideal for generating profit and consumer value simultaneously.

Store two is located at the opposite end of the mall. Unlike the first store, it has an overstated elegance. Its sales people are like models from a fashion show. The store appears to be expensive and formal. Its "special" sales are not quite convincing. The store also has its distinguishing features, but these characteristics are not quite appealing to their perspective customers. Store two has been struggling mostly because it's lacking differential congruence.

Thus, differential congruence means that the retail establishment has certain distinguishing features that are not only expected, but are also well accepted. Any successful retail establishment has certain features that are liked by its customers. Because of these features, customers come back and continue patronizing that store. Even if some of the retail establishments that are offering similar products and services that appear to be quite similar, such as some of the fast food places or low-price convenience store, in reality, they have some features that are quite different than others such as location, personnel, or some special services. These differences in their offering are valued by their customers and that is why they continue to visit the retail establishment.

In our market system, which is primarily described as a prevailing monopolistic competition where each and every establishment is unique, every retail establishment is a monopolistic competitor. Managing uniqueness and making it most appealing are the key tenets of proactive and successful retail management activity. This is all about differential congruence. In order to achieve differential congruence, first we must establish retailing goals and, second, we must manage retailing mixes.

ESTABLISHING RETAILING GOALS

Establishing goals for a retail establishment is very critical. As I stated in my previous book: "if we don't know where we are going, how can we get there?" This is an orientation that is reinforced throughout this book. The reader or the retailer to be must have critical and achievable goals in mind. Naturally, these goals must be realistic enough to put the retailer in the right path to achieve the desirable market presence. When Sears established the goals of good value for the American middle class, they did very well for many years. When Walmart aimed at the lower middle class with cheap prices and delivered what it promoted it did very well. Then Bulgart, a well-known jewelry retailer, delivers uniquely designed jewelry to the very rich of the world, and does extremely well. When Wendy's aims at natural markets with its hamburgers and other fast foods, it also does very well. This list could go on indefinitely.

It must be noted that all of these cases display a very close connection between their goals and their delivery. Just how does a retailer, regardless of size, establish goals? Furthermore, do these goals remain the same in time?

Although there are many different ways of establishing goals, there are many different goal options. Knowing the market quite well is perhaps the key to all or, at least, to most alternatives in establishing goals. If the retailer knows the market well then it becomes possible to think of new opportunities based on what consumers in a given area may need and yet, are not receiving. In an area, for example, where average income is high and golfing is big, expensive golfing equipment retailing does well. In an adjacent area, however, where the average income is not so high, but aspirations of consumers imitate the expensive lifestyle are high, used golfing equipment and golfing shoe repair may be a very good goal to pursue. Similarly, there may be an obvious gap in the supply and demand of health food or electronic equipment. These may create great retailing opportunities. When my friend opened a souvlaki place adjacent to a major university, he took advantage of the students who were tired of hamburgers and pizzas, but had no other alternatives. He is now a rather rich man. Having special skills that may be useful or needed by consumers is a very good plus factor. A good, short-order cook may develop certain dishes that may be very popular, say, with students in a college town. Similarly, working with a franchising company and using its expertise to get a small retail establishment started is a commonly used goal-development activity. Major franchising companies have their own retailing goals that can be localized rather easily by a franchise and may give a future entrepreneur a good start. But, knowing where to go is far different from getting there. The retailer must use the special features or tools that the retail store has developed. These features are basic, controllable factors that develop and manipulate the retail image and market it suitable to the target market. In other words, develop and strengthen the differential congruence. Thus, the retailer becomes successful as the retail store generates customer value.

MANAGING THE RETAIL MARKETING MIXES

There are five retail marketing mixes at the retailer's disposal that can be used as tools to implement the overall retail strategy. These retail mixes are: the goals and services mix, the communications mix, the pricing mix, the human resource mix, and the logistic mix, as shown in Exhibit 2.1. Although all of these are discussed separately in detail in this book, a brief discussion of each is in order, here.

The goods and services mix gives the retailer its reason to exist. The merchandise assortment is by far the key identifying feature of a retail establishment. Payless Shoe Source is known for its limited variety and extremely low prices. Target is known for its reasonable prices and extensive variety of reasonably good-quality merchandise. Taco Bell is known for low-priced Mexican food dishes. This list can go on until the last retailer is mentioned. Along with the merchandise, a retail store also offers services. Apple stores are very well known for

Exhibit 2.1   Retailing Mixes

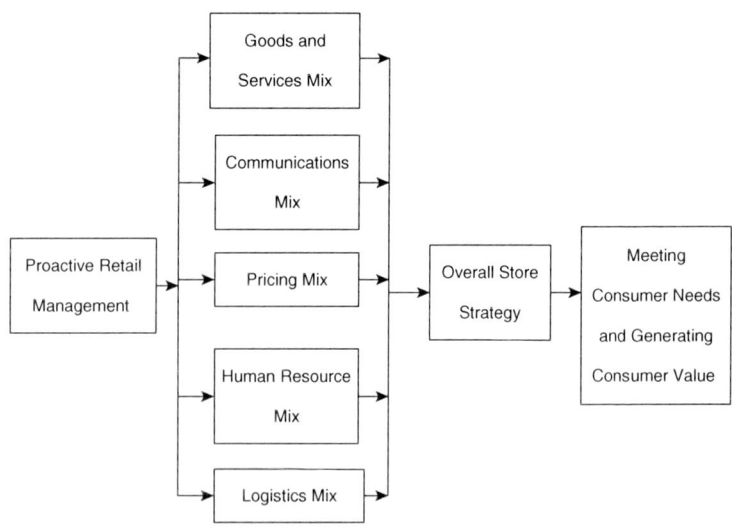

Source: Adapted and revised from Samli (2004).

that feature. If the merchandise mix is right, services typically play a synergistic role by complementing it and raising its appeal and the satisfaction it generates.

The communication mix is the way the retailer informs its prospective customers and keeps in touch with its regular customers. No retail establishment can survive and prosper without some promotion. Being a well-kept secret for a retailer is totally unacceptable. Many small retailers, particularly in small communities, assume that "word of mouth" type of promotion is more than adequate and that they don't need additional advertising or promotion. This invariably becomes useless and the retailer fails. The communication mix in addition to a multimedia component which includes advertising, personal selling, sales promotion, and the internet in recent years, has added social media as part of the communication mix. This is a major addition that is discussed in a different section of this book.

The pricing mix has three critical components: efficiency, competition, and image. The first implies the management styles of running the retail establishment. If the establishment is run efficiently, the savings will be passed onto the store's customers through lower prices and perhaps with increased services. The competitiveness component indicates that the retail establishment uses price as its major competitive tool. Discount stores, bargain basements, outlet stores, buying clubs, and other similar retail operations use price for that purpose. Many of these discount-oriented establishments emphasize the policy of "we will not be undersold knowingly." Finally, the image component means the store is using its price mix to promote an image of being a reasonable place with some exceptional offerings and overall, being a place where one would save. However, such a strategy calls for carefully planned pricing practices without creating price wars with competitors or being a "cheap" place which is not really providing good consumer value.

The human resource mix, particularly for small or medium-sized retailers, is a competitive tool. This is where the relationship marketing begins. Specifically, a small or medium-sized retailer without a friendly, talkative, knowledgeable, and understanding group of employees who are ready and anxious to serve their customers cannot possibly succeed. The retailing people must have information and empathy for the consumer needs and must be able to make a positive effort to satisfy the needs of their customers. This is true for selling and nonselling personnel of retail establishments. If the human resources of the retail establishment go out of their way to help customers in every way necessary, those customers will come back again and again. Furthermore, they will bring others along with them.

The logistics mix has two key and distinct components: in-store logistics and out-of-store logistics. In-store logistics provide proper merchandise, combinations in the right places in the store, moving the merchandise subtly from the storage to where it is displayed for sale, and making sure that merchandise is made easy to find. These are just some of the extremely critical in store activities for retail success. Out-of-store logistics means having a quick response system on the part of the retailer, activating and supporting the merchandise mix. Receiving merchandise or replenishing what is needed in the most cost- and time-efficient manner is a key function of this activity. These two aspects of logistics must be kept in balance for optimal results.

SYNERGY AMONG THE MIXES

Retailing, in essence, is constructing an image and managing it by reinforcing, by strengthening, and by modifying, if necessary. All of the five mixes discussed here are part of the store image. All of the activities that are performed by the five mixes have a direct and indirect impact on the overall store image management. Whether the image is being developed, maintained, or modified, it is important for the retailer to make sure that the components of all five mixes are working together. Otherwise, they may nullify each other, and the store may perform submarginally. Consider, for instance, Winn Dixie. As a large grocery store chain, it was trying to be a major provider of beef and also reasonably low-priced groceries. But, both of these appeals did not register with consumers and the chain got into a major financial trouble. The chain was purchased by another company. Whether or not the new management would be able to develop certain uniqueness in Winn Dixie and coordinate these features by customers' needs remains to be seen. It must be understood that the market has memory, so it does not forget and does not forgive easily. Lack of congruence among the retail mix components can create not only suboptimal performance, but also undesirable memories. But, if the retail mixes are working well but the retail establishment is aiming at the wrong target market, this means it is lacking the understanding of *differential congruence*, which is deadly.

IMAGE MANAGEMENT IS THE KEY

As can be seen, developing and managing the store image can be equated to the overall retail marketing management. Customers going to Cartier's, Neiman Marcus, or Walmart know what to expect, and they therefore make a deliberate choice. The retailer must make sure that it is that deliberate choice which is expected to take place when the store image is managed properly: that is the store is projecting an image that is confirmed by its strategic retail management.

The store image is obviously critical. It represents what the retail store is all about. All aspects of communication that the store performs through its retail mix in a market and aim particularly at certain targets; regardless, these targets are regular market segments or emerge niche markets and play a critical role in the composition and the maintenance of that image. It must be reiterated that the store image which is the sum total of all of the impressions about a store, is synergistic. It has numerous components such as appearance, sales people's attitudes, merchandise mix, internal layout, and many others. But, the store image, as a result of synergism, is more than the sum total of all of these individual elements.

Regardless of whether the image is existing or in the making, it is the key in formulating an implementation of the store's strategy. If the store is aiming at the older and well-to-do segments in the market, a dynamic, youthful image is not likely to do the job. To illustrate, the Glow-Wood Restaurant was located adjacent to a major metropolitan university. It was kept open 24 hours a day, seven days a week. It catered primarily to students and unskilled blue-collar workers residing in that particular community. A good atmosphere of communication and relaxation prevailed in the restaurant. Food was cheap and waitresses were friendly. The restaurant was always crowded and was very successful. When the owners retired, they sold it. The new owner wanted to make the restaurant an elegant, high-class place. He changed the interior, the menu, and the appearance of the establishment. In less than six months, he was out of business. The elegant image he tried to create was not acceptable to the existing market segment. The regular customers did not feel comfortable in the new setting that he created (Samli 2004).

It is not possible to modify or change the marketing strategy without paying attention to the existing image and the market in which the current operations are taking place. Here, it is critical to identify two types of images: intended and perceived. For a successful retail establishment, these two must be the same. Consider the following: a bank in the Midwest considered itself to be the elite or upscale bank in the community, catering to the upper-middle and upper socioeconomic classes. It had been promoting an image accordingly. The services it offered were more expensive than typical banks. Its interior layout was rather plush. However, research undertaken by the nearby university indicated that the bank actually was catering to the lower-middle class. Its customers didn't care for all the frills that the bank offered. The discrepancy between the intended and actual image in this case is rather clear. The bank was wasting a lot of money and effort trying to project an image that was not acceptable. If the intended actual images are not the same, the expected customer satisfaction-driven customer loyalty cannot be achieved. Exhibit 2.2 illustrates three degrees of relationships between the intended and the actual store images. It clearly reiterates that the intended and actual images of the retail establishment must be one and the same for the firm to optimize its performance.

However, even if the intended and actual images are the same, how the retailer arrived at this point is critical. From this perspective, the retailer has three options. The retail establishment might have arrived that point proactively which is the most desirable approach. Alternatively, the retailer may try to reach that point by simply being reactive and not doing much and finally striving for the point of equality in images may be done simply by being inactive. This last point simply indicates that for some reason the retailer was not striving perhaps to even survive or did not know any better.

Developing the right kind of image proactively implies that the retailer makes a clear-cut decision about its goals, goes after the specified goals with a proactive strategy, and succeeds. Such a strategic orientation most of the time leads to success. Being the best jeweler or the best Chinese restaurant in a given market area are examples of such goals and accomplishments.

Exhibit 2.2   The Workings of Differential Congruence

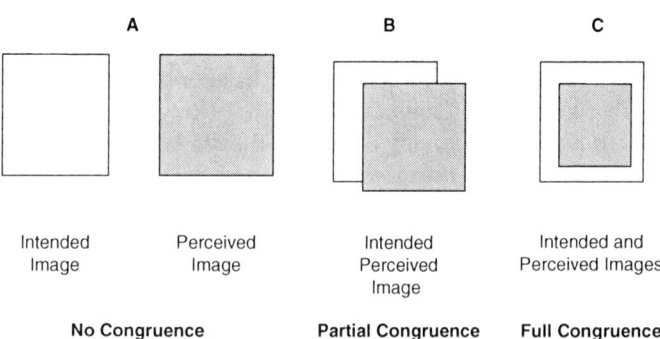

A	B	C
Intended Image	Perceived Image	Intended Perceived Image	Intended and Perceived Images
No Congruence	**Partial Congruence**	**Full Congruence**

Note: Full congruence implies that the management of the store and the store's consumers are all in sync.

Source: Adapted and revised from Samli, 2004.

Developing the right kind of image reactively implies that although the retailer wanted to be the best jeweler in the specific market, it is not being perceived as such. It is perceived, perhaps, as the place that is quite reasonable and offers good value. That retailer needs to change its intended image and must adjust the retail mix strategies accordingly. If this adjustment is not made, much will be lost in terms of market positioning and profitability. If this retailer does not display consistency between its intended image and perceived image in time, it may not survive.

Although it may be simply pure luck, even though the retailer may not have a specific goal and a plan of action, it may manage to survive for a while. This retailer may be perceived by the market as not having any key claims, but it is doing a reasonable job for the time being. It certainly is not counting on having loyal customers who would make survival and profitability possible.

Needless to say, proactive image building and striving for consistency between the intended image and perceived image, meaning that the store is achieving differential congruence, create greater market power and resultant profit. Many retailers, unfortunately, fall into the category of being inactive and hence, many of them fail.

SUMMARY

Retail marketing strategy is extremely critical for survival. Every retailer must have a game plan to fulfill its goals and generate customer value, which is the essence of profitability. This game plan is the retail strategy. In order to develop a successful retail marketing strategy, the retailer must understand the theory of differential congruence. In other words, the retailer must know what its unique features are and what its customers expect. If there is congruence here and if through congruence the retailer becomes quite different than others, then that retail establishment is heading in the right direction. Congruence must be differential, indicating the uniqueness of that retail operation.

In order to develop differential congruence, the retail establishment must have some specific goals regarding its target audiences and a strategy to achieve them. The retailer uses five groups of strategic tools to develop a strategy. These groups of tools are called retail mixes. These are the five retail mixes: goods and services, communications, pricing, human resources, and logistics. If all of these mixes work together, the retailer will optimize the overall performance by creating customer value and maximizing profits.

3

FITTING INTO MULTILAYERED RETAIL COMPETITION

Saks Fifth Avenue competes with Neiman Marcus rather directly, but even indirectly it does not reflect the business Dollar Tree stores, a chain of super discount stores. On the other hand, because of the accessibility of the retailing facilities and variety of these offerings and because of the mobility of customers and their access to retailing information, in a general sense all retailers are competing with each other.

In order to survive and succeed in the retailing sector, it is important to understand the nature and intensity of retail competition. In the retail jungle there are six distinct layers of retail competition. Any retailers and any retailer to be must be very familiar with all of these layers and must understand how each impacts the particular establishment in question. Placing oneself in the right layer implies understanding the nature of the competition a retailer must be equipped to face.

Exhibit 3.1 illustrates the layers of retail competition from the most basic nuts and bolts type of competition to the broadest market competition. Each layer indicates a different type of retail competition that one needs to understand if one wants to survive in the retail jungle. As can be seen, our discussion deals with six layers.

LEVEL ONE

This is the most common type of competition. Every retailer must offer a combination of its five mixes. This is how it survives and succeeds. But all retailers cannot offer such a positive and proactive combination of their mixes. This is partly because some simply don't know what needs to be done and others are short of resources. But it must be reiterated that those that can put together the best combination for their target markets are those who are likely to

Exhibit 3.1 Levels of Retail Competition

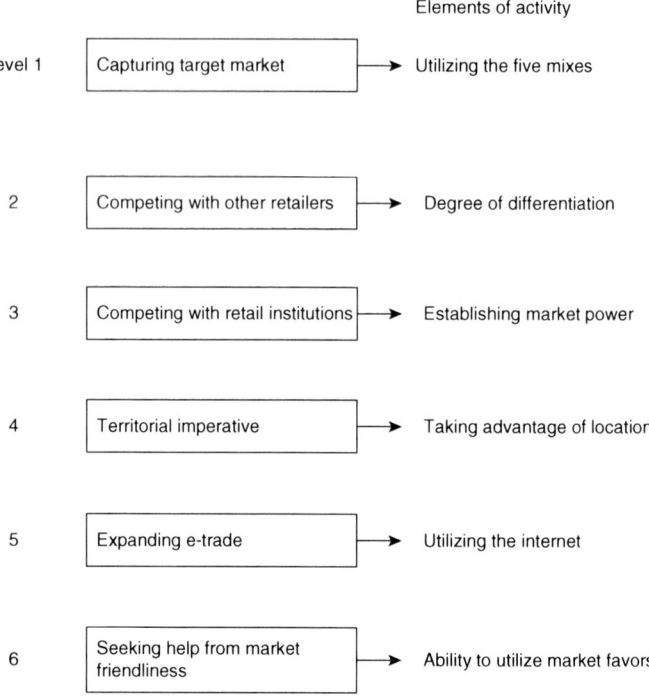

succeed. There, among other considerations, the *turnover classification theory* comes into play. Those products that have high turnover rates, which means in a given period they are sold more often, are typically categorized as convenience products that are consumed or purchased very often. Here, their prices need to be low; hence, they have low markup levels. They contribute to the wellbeing of the retail store by large volume sales. Exhibit 3.2 illustrates four scenarios. The upper-left quadrant of the exhibit shows a rather unlikely situation dealing with a high turnover, high markup situation. This is an exceptional occurrence where, for a short period of time, some special products may be very much in demand. Certain fashion goods or some regularly used products not readily available could generate such a situation.

The lower-left quadrant indicates the normal case of high markup and low turnover. Typically, luxury items and some other conveniences available such as appliances, cars, and computers, belong in this category.

Exhibit 3.2   Markup and Turnover Classification

Markup levels

High	Low
Special short-lasting products	
Fashion goods	Convenience products
Limited supply	Consumer nondurable groceries
Products	
Luxury items	Introductory products
Expensive products	Some shopping good
Jewelry, expensive cars	Some pharmaceutical

The upper-right-hand corner also indicates the standard condition. Products with low markup typically have high turnover rates. Most convenience products are in that category. 7-Eleven stores thrive on such merchandise mix characteristics.

Finally, the lower-right quadrant displays the most difficult scenario. Having low markup while having a low turnover is not a sustainable situation. Products in this situation cannot remain in existence for a long time. Certainly if the retailer is experiencing this situation for most of the products in the store, something dramatic must take place such as a totally different marketing strategy based on a new product mix. Of course, it must be kept in mind that this scenario is a possibility for some of the introductory products that may be expected to gain momentum in the market place.

Although department stores or discount stores carry products that fall into each of the four categories illustrated in Exhibit 3.2, there is also a national tendency for products to be grouped, which basically means retailers are categorized based on the product group they primarily emphasize. The critical point to remember here is that truly luxury product retailers do not go near a group of lower-priced convenience-oriented product retailers or vice versa. Hirschman (1979) coined this basic principle as the *network dominance theory*, which states that naturally certain groups of retailers must cluster so that they attract certain specified consumer groups. For example, Bloomingdale's carries products and brands that are of good quality and that are somewhat higher priced; it competes with, say, Neiman Marcus and, therefore, it may be located somewhere near it. But if it were to be located next to a barbershop, it may not be appropriate for consumers; similarly, if it were to be located next to Payless Shoe

Source or a Chinese take-out restaurant, it may not be appropriate. Indeed, instead a Cartier store will have to locate near Saks Fifth Avenue. This indicates that there is a priority ordering in a grouping of retail establishments. Exhibit 3.3 illustrates some details of the natural dominance theory.

According to natural dominance theory, not only is it important to group retail stores, but also there is a priority ordering in the groupings of these retail establishments. Again, next to Neiman Marcus, there may be a Saks Fifth Avenue, and similarly, there may be an expensive jewelry store or decorative home accessories outlet, but they are all upscale and grouped together.

In the middle groups of Exhibit 3.3, there may be a Sears surrounded by Victoria's Secret, Limited Express, and the like. In terms of product categories, staples, soft goods, books, appliances, and consumer electronics are likely to be brought together in this group. Obviously, this group represents reasonable prices with acceptable quality.

Exhibit 3.3   Natural Dominance Theory

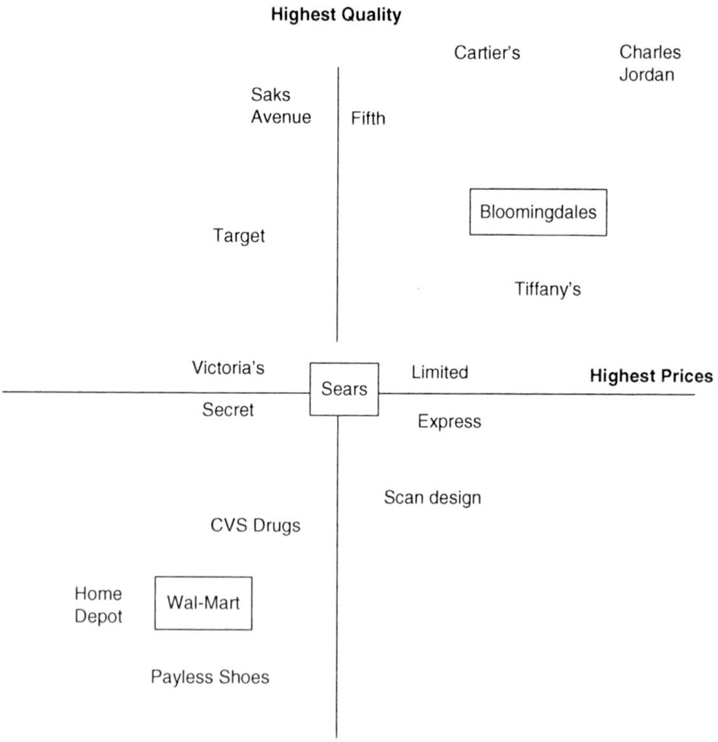

By the same token, in a low- to middle-class setting, one would find a Walmart surrounded by CVS drugs, Payless Shoe Source, and Home Depot, among others, grouped together. Product groupings in this case may be convenience store goods, home improvement supplies, fast foods, health, and beauty aids, as well as groceries.

Natural dominance theory would basically apply to all five of the six retail competition levels. The social media and e-trade activity can and perhaps, should be at all levels. However, this category is identified as a separate level of retail competition levels. In Exhibit 3.1, it really exists and is used at all levels of retail competition. On the basis of natural dominance theory, it is essential to realize that a barber shop would not do well if it were next to, say, Bloomingdale's, but it would do well next to a place like McDonald's.

It is critical to realize that between the Natural dominance theory and the Turnover classification theories, many retailing successes and failures can at least partially be explained. They are the overwhelming force behind the location decisions.

Victoria's: A Short Example

Victoria's was an elegant retailing store, somewhat classy and a little bit pricey. It was a store of women's apparel and accessories. The owner of the store wanted to locate at a high traffic area; hence, the store was located next to a large Kroger supermarket. There was also a drugstore, ice cream parlor, and McDonald's adjacent to Victoria's. The traffic created this group of stores, particularly Kroger's, which were not what Victoria's needed. People who went to the supermarket to shop casually were not in the mood to visit a somewhat classy and formal apparel store. Unfortunately, the owner-manager of Victoria's did not know much about Natural dominance theory. This was not a good location for Victoria's. Because of this, Victoria's went out of existence in about a year.

Level Two

Exhibit 3.1 describes this level as "competing with other retailers." At any given time in population centers such as cities or towns or suburban areas, many retail establishments that are similar to each other are competing. Sears, Target, Kroger, Winn-Dixie, McDonald's, and Burger King are among these.

All of these stores are involved in attempting to develop competitive advantage or differential congruence and compete with each other (Samli 2004). There may be at least four generic forms of competition at this level. These are all intra-institutional ways of developing competitive advantage that translate into differential congruence. These four generic forms of competition are: imitation, deviation, complementation, and innovation (Samli 2004). The following is a brief description of these four generic competitive practices.

Imitation

As seen in Exhibit 3.3, all retailers have certain traditional lines of merchandising that are known by their customers which are regularly followed by these retailers. Carrying certain basic merchandise mix, therefore, is logical and necessary. A basic inventory that will appeal to the "core" market is a must. From that perspective, if one were to analyze the depth and breadth of inventories of offerings carried by Walmart and Costco or the menus offered by McDonald's and Burger King, one may not find significant differences. The core markets here are similar, especially for larger retailers. Hence, it is natural that their merchandise or service mixes overlap.

Many small retailers also use imitation as a method of competition. In such cases, small retailers that do have a clear-cut mission or a well-defined target market may imitate the large retailer that has been successful in that market so that it can stay in business by taking away a small part of the large retailer's business. For example, a shoe store that is located next to a Target store following the same type of conditions that Target has, but with a larger variety of shoes. It will pick up a part of Target's traffic by having a narrower but deeper inventory.

Deviation

Despite the fact that many retailers imitate each other at their core activity, they also deviate from each other in practice. This deviation differentiates the retailer and identifies it in terms of its uniqueness. Deviation, just as imitation, is also exercised by the use of retail mixes. As implied earlier, all five of the mixes contribute to the retailer's overall image. Thus, even Walmart and Costco overlap in 80 percent of their activities, while the 20 percent of difference would at least distinguish the two from each other. In fact, this 20 percent is extremely critical for managing and catering to their somewhat different clients. Although grocery chains such as Publix, Fresh Market, and Winn-Dixie may overlap about 85 percent, one may have more local produce, the other may have greater emphasis on health foods or gourmet lines. Thus, the 15 percent deviation may be extremely critical for them to establish their identity.

Complementation

Many consumer products are sold most readily when the choice offered is greater and when that choice is supported with other products and services complementing it. This particular principle is critical in retailing shopping goods. Consumers here would like to have more alternatives so that they can more readily shop around for better quality and price—in short, better buys or bargains. That means having more options to choose from is preferable. This is why the stores, as mentioned earlier in discussing natural superiority theory, gather together not only to compete, but also to create complementation—in other words, greater choices for consumers. An ice cream parlor that is selling somewhat exotic flavors and a large variety of ice cream near a gourmet restaurant may do well since after a big meal many customers may desire a refreshing finish. This is complementation.

Innovation

In the final analysis, retail establishments compete with all comers through their innovativeness by generating differential advantage. The retail establishment, by carrying unique merchandise or by handling the well-known merchandise differently, by serving their customers in more unconventional ways, or even having personnel that behave differently, can manage its name and its image more uniquely than its competitors. A few years ago, Pizza Hut's "eating the pizza the wrong way" campaign and McDonald's giving-away beanie babies when they were very popular were innovative behaviors. More recently, Apple stores have been very successful by both selling newly innovated products as well as providing super-quality service. Although innovative competition carries more risk and higher cost factors, there is also a greater opportunity to establish or enhance the store's competitive advantage. Similarly, Apple stores have shown that understanding and utilizing technological advances can be an important part of this innovation process.

Of these four generic competitive practices, small retailers may be more inclined to go into imitation or complementation, since these are easier and less costly avenues. However, more entrepreneurial and creative retailers may go for innovation. Although relatively more risky than others, this option is likely to be more profitable. Understanding these four generic competitive practices and choosing one deliberately is likely to put the retailer into a more powerful competitive stance.

LEVEL THREE

The third level of retail competition as presented in Exhibit 3.1 is competing with retail institutions. Inter-institutional retailing is rather common in our market economy. That means many different types of retailers are competing for the same result of survival and profitability. Different types of retail establishments have emerged on the American scene during the past three decades or so. Many of them manage to survive and coexist.

Exhibit 3.4 lists some of these retail establishments and identifies their strategic powers. This is how inter-institutional competition in

Exhibit 3.4   Retail Mixes as Strategic Tools*

Type of Retailer	Location	Product Mix	Service	Personnel	Pomotion	Prices	Logistics
Convenience Stores (7–11, Gate, etc.)	+	–	–	–	–	–	–
Supermarket (Kroger, Publix, etc.)	+	+	+	+	+	+	+
Discount Stores (Wal-Mart, Costco, etc.)	–	+	–	+	+	+	+
Box (Limited Line) Store (Jewel T)	+	–	–	–	+	+	+
Warehouse Store (Sam's, Target, etc.)	–	–	–	–	+	+	+
Specialty Stores (The Limited, Gap, etc.)	+	+	+	+	+	+	–
Supercenter (Safeway, Best Buys)	+	+	–	–	+	+	+
E-Tailers	+	+	–	–	+	+	–

(+ = advantage, – = neutral or disadvantage)
*Although typically goods and service mix is the general management tool, in this diagram the two were separated for special impact.
Although location is not a retail mix, once it is decided upon it becomes a given. However, comparing different recall institutions, location plays a significant role as a competitive tool.

Source: Adapted and revised from Samli 2004.

retailing works. As can be seen in the exhibits, some of these retail institutions have only one advantage: price. Box stores and warehouse stores along with discounters exclusively emphasize price. But specialty stores such as The Limited or Gap have more pluses. This is why they are so resilient and despite increasingly unfriendly conditions in the market place, they manage to survive.

Supercenters, which are conveniently located and offer low-price, high-variety retail facilities that concentrate on one-stop shopping, may become more of a threat than others. They seem to be attracting customers from distances as far as 100 miles away (Leah 1995; Flikinger 1995; Samli 1998). For small retailers, all of the five mixes must be carefully considered and used. This, of course, makes small retailing management very challenging. All six mixes must be carefully planned and used if particularly small retailers want to survive the retail jungle.

LEVEL FOUR

The fourth level illustrated in Exhibit 3.1 deals with geographic superiority or territorial imperative of the retailer. In level three natural dominance discussions relate to the particular location of the retailer. In level four the particular location is emphasized as the place where the retailer is located and can easily be construed as the most important factor in retail survival. This special dimension of retailing has three key dimensions: location of the town where the store is, location of the shopping complex in which the retail store is positioned, and the actual location of the store itself.

The Town

Location of town typically relates to out-shopping. People who live in Small Town A may go many miles to shop at Larger Town B because of selection of merchandise, more attractive prices, and even perhaps the pleasure of shopping. Clearly, the town in which the retail establishment is located is a significant consideration. Some cities or towns are more dynamic and provide a better overall market potential for the retail store. On the other hand, the town or even the city may be a sleepy one, meaning, primarily, not having a proactive retailing sector. Some people there may be quite satisfied with the status quo, but others may be quite unhappy with the retail facilities and their offerings that exist in the town. The overall sets of alternatives, the services, the prices, accessibility of retail establishments, and parking, among other considerations, could be quite unacceptable. It is critical for the retailer to understand the difference between these two opposing conditions and adjust its overall strategy accordingly.

The Shopping Complexes

The concept of territorial imperative comes more into focus when there are identifiable patronage preferences exhibited or expressed toward a given shopping complex in which the individual retail store may consider locating or is already located. This particular shopping complex could be a major shopping center, a cluster, a group of retailers in the form of a string, regional mall, or downtown, among others. Each one of these alternatives would have its own strengths and weaknesses that our retail establishment must consider carefully before locating there. These strengths and weaknesses must be reevaluated periodically because, in time, such features change.

If customers, for a series of special reasons, prefer to go to a particular shopping complex and become loyal to it, this loyalty spills over to all of the stores in that complex. The retail establishments in the complex present a synergistic front. If our retail establishment can locate on a complex of this type and manage to fit in, it will certainly benefit from this synergistic front that attracts many customers.

It is critical to realize that a retailer at any given time has multiple location options and, hence, must realize that location is a critical retail variable tool. This variable tool is particularly important before retail operations commence. Once the retail establishment becomes an ongoing operation, it is too late to take advantage of multiple site options. When it is obvious that the present location is no longer functional, then the retailer may have to quickly choose a better site.

Specific Site of Our Store

In addition to the town itself and the location of the shopping complex, the specific site chosen for our store is obviously very critical. Consider, for instance, a neighborhood fast food store or an ice cream parlor. Those and other similar types of stores may not have many distinguishing features and all by themselves they may not have much appeal to bring customers in. But, because of very favorable location selection, they may be able to establish a competitive advantage. If they can fulfill their target market needs, their stores can generate substantial profits. They develop their own competitive advantage and generate profit as they create consumer value. As can be seen, this special dimension of retailing could easily yield competitive advantage that would lead to differential congruence.

Ability to choose good locations becomes even more critical for multiunit retailers such as Target, Walmart, International House of Pancakes, or Holiday Inn must have specific location criteria that will generate optimal results. Imagine what happens if Charles Jordan ends up locating next to a barbershop or Bulgari Jewelers locates next to a Dollar Tree store that sells odds and ends all priced at one dollar. All of the units in such chains must show consistency in terms of proximity to other stores and informs of the economic and social features of their chosen locations. Again, it is rather obvious that small retailers, unlike discount giants, do not have the luxury of using a free-standing location. By definition, small and medium-sized retailers must locate in attractive locations because they cannot draw large groups of consumers. But, they can accommodate large groups if these groups are already there.

One last point relating to retail chains, it is my personal opinion that when locations are chosen and retailing activity is in full bloom, store closings could become a serious error. As this book is being written, Radio-Shack and Staples are closing numerous stores because those individual units are not making money. If the chain, as a whole, is successful it would be wrong to close down a number of their stores. It is not totally essential that each and every unit should be satisfactorily profitable. Closing stores can have a very strong, negative message to the whole country that cannot be corrected by local advertising. Rash financial decisions such as closing down hundreds of units of the chain must be avoided. They become an extremely negative marketing activity.

LEVEL FIVE

In recent years, there has been a significant increase in e-tailing or retailing through the Internet. Although it is a small proportion of total retailing volume, e-tailing is increasing. In fact, many retailers, large and small, are developing the capability to sell online. Even if the store is not selling a large volume through the Internet, it's communicating with its customers or potential customers through the Internet. Although mistakenly, some retailers have gone exclusively online and have not done very well. But, the retailers who have added the Internet as an additional way of communicating with their customers and encouraging them to patron their place of business have been doing quite well. With the development of smartphones, consumers are able to search for local information such as a local store they want to visit. Large numbers of consumers are engaged in looking up prices of a store's mobile site and many of them are able to check inventory prior to shopping in the store (local and e-tailing group 2012). The retailers who are improving this two-way electronic communication are likely to be in a more advantageous position than their competitors.

LEVEL SIX

This level describes the prevailing retail competition in the broadest possible manner. The retailing sector, despite its tendencies to become more oligopolistic, is still, in essence, a good example of monopolistic competition. Here, all establishments are unique in their own way, with no two exactly alike because of their merchandise mix, logistics mix, locating, layout, and other unique features. Every retail establishment has a certain degree of monopoly power based on its uniqueness. Because of this monopoly power, the retail establishment can create a degree of differential congruence which is the essence of survival and profit. Within reason, the economic power created by differential congruence means loyal customers may pay a little more for the products that the retailer is offering rather than switching to another store. However, these conditions depend on the type of store and the type of merchandise and services it offers. The customers of Gucci or Bulgari are more likely to be loyal to these stores than customers of Walmart or 7–11. Though this power should not be abused, Gucci can raise its prices and get away with it. On the other hand, it will be rather difficult, if not impossible, for Walmart to raise its prices because it does not have much monopoly power. Its customers will not be loyal if Walmart were to increase its prices.

Although lack of information or the prevailing lack of rationality can tempt the retailer to advertise and promote more to convince the consumers about, say, the best prices that are available there, such claims should not be outrageously out of line. Otherwise, the whole activity can be useless or even self-destructive. If the claims of the retailer are not believable, then those claims create a credibility gap and make conditions worse for the retail store. Thus, the skills to achieve competitive advantage, or to go how far one can go and where one must stop, are not simply skills that all retailers are born with. In fact, those skills require know-how information and experience. While some retailers have these skills instinctively and some others acquire them rather quickly, many other retailers may never possess them and they cease to exist. Successful retailing strategy is necessary to meet and exceed retail competition at all of the six levels that are presented in this chapter.

SUMMARY

Retail competition is very keen and it happens in at least six distinct levels. This chapter presents a discussion for all of these six levels. Starting with the very specific and going to the broadest levels of retail competition, an attempt is made to describe them. These six levels are all retailed to competition through retail mixes. The individual retailer must understand these different levels of competition and must have an idea as to how to behave in each level.

This chapter presents two important retail competition theories. The first is margin versus turnover interaction and the second is natural dominance theory. Both are rather important in judging the chances of survival for a retail establishment.

The chapter treats retail location decisions under the title of territorial imperative. The importance of and options in the retail location decision must be considered very seriously.

The recent development on the use and support of the Internet is touched upon. This is a very critical and dynamic area to explore closely.

Finally, a critical discussion is presented regarding the nature of the economic conditions within which retailer functions. It must be reiterated that the retailer must be cognizant of all of these levels of competition and how a retail establishment should behave in each. This is not saying that all the competition is within each level only. On the contrary, there is always significant competition between the levels as well. It is up to the individual retailer to decide which aspect of competition is more critical and how to cope with it for survival and success.

4

Major trends in the Retailing Sector Which Independents Must Know

A retailer must be aware of national as well as local trends and must be able to cope; better yet, if possible, to keep ahead of these developments. The smaller the retail establishment, however, the less important national trends are. It is quite likely that national trends may not quite reach to small neighborhoods. However, they do generate a trickle effect. Retail establishments, particularly small retailers, must be more aware of local conditions such as a major change in the local highway system that would redirect local vehicular traffic and change the traffic on which local retailers rely. Similarly, the announcement of a major discount retailer locating outside of town or the change in the town's development plans, say, from east side to west side, may be more critical to local small retailers than the stock market crash or a recession in the national economy. This does not mean that local small retailers should not know or, worse yet, not understand national trends. It simply means that retailers must be aware of local conditions that may have an immediate impact on their performance.

The Greek Restaurant Case

In order to elaborate on the above statement, the following can be cited. A uniquely organized Greek restaurant was having difficulty surviving. The owner-manager kept on saying that the national recession is destroying his business. But a restaurant needs only a few hundred customers, which, most likely, has nothing to do with the national economic conditions. The manager did not establish enough contact with the customers and the restaurant went out of business. If the manager knew what the real reason for local people not frequenting his restaurant, some remedial steps could have been taken.

This situation becomes more serious if the national economic trends are misinterpreted. As this book is being written, Radio Shack announced that it was closing up to 1,000 of its stores and Staples stated that it will close 225 of its stores. Both organizations claimed the "Internet age" market dominance will not be achieved by building more brick-and-mortar stores. They claim that customers are not spending the way they used to. The shopper visits are down and on-line shopping is increasing. The managements of these and other retail chains are thinking of closing units that are not performing well; however, they must know that the total shopping through the Internet is simply not much above 5 percent of the national total retail sales. Having what the consumers would like cannot be solved by a brisk and thoughtless financial decision of closing hundreds of stores. These companies must improve their retailing strategies. In a market economy, functioning with the dictates of finances could be deadly for retail chains.

Thus, understanding the national trends and coping with them is more of a critical consideration for a large-scale retailer. However, this does not mean that local small retailers should not be concerned with or, worse yet, not understand national trends. It simply means that small retailers must be more aware of local conditions that may have an immediate impact on their functional proficiency.

What Is Important In Retailing Nationally

Perhaps the most important national trend with a very significant impact on retailing is that today's consumer has a tremendous amount of information obtained from social media such as YouTube, Facebook, and the like. This information, which is connecting consumers with each other rather than consumers' receiving messages through mass media, may become very critical for retailing. Although the volume of actual sales through the Internet is not very high, the utilization of the information received through the social media in terms of making purchase decisions is very high. As discussed in different sections of this book, this is one area small and medium-sized independent retailers could excel and do a better job than the discount giants by properly using the information generated by the modern electronic capabilities.

The second major national trend is the resurgence of wholesale discount outlets; these are also named as warehouse stores such as Costco, Sam's, and BJ's. These establishments provide a tremendous variety of products at low prices. They do not present a very attractive retail ambiance; however, they are very popular. They are expanding and are likely to continue to do so.

The third major trend is discounting. In fact, discounting has become so widespread that it would be reasonable to call the current times as the era of discounting. Discount department stores such as Walmart and Target are performing much better than traditional department stores. Perhaps it is critical to note that in recent years Walmart has expanded its operations into grocery retailing as well. This move not only radically reformulates the grocery retailing sector, but also reiterates the power of discounting.

After a period of more than a decade of decrease in the number of retail stores per 1,000 population, this number has started to increase again. However, this increase is primarily in the small and mid-sized retailing areas. This is the fourth major trend.

Old, reputable, high-class retail establishments carrying luxury products not only have remained in business comfortably, but also expanded their activities. They capture a remarkable proportion of the market.

Finally, franchising, particularly in fast food and low-price retailing, has been increasing. This is a dynamic area and is making good progress. However, organizations, such as Chick-Fil-A, Burger King, and Wendy's, are lowering the price and making what has been referred to as commoditization, or called in some circles as McDonaldization. In other words, they are putting particular emphasis on pricing and trying to make a profit by increased volume (Berman and Evans 2012).

Retailers must follow and learn to interpret these trends. They may modify their practices to adjust to them and improve their own probability of survival and success. Exhibit 4.1 illustrates all six important retailing trends and gives some reasoning behind each.

E-tailing or "clicks" as it is referred to in retailing practice has increased in volume because of the convenience it offers to those who may not be very mobile or to those who are extremely busy consumers, and certainly to those who are extremely attached to their computers. The growth of e-trade and certain predictions about its future are somewhat exaggerated.

Numerous small retailers closed down their "brick and mortar" businesses and went online and did not do very well. It is maintained here that a balanced approach to "brick and mortar" and "clicking" is the best way, not one or the other. In the late 1990s some ill-fated retailers who thought they could continue retailing without having "brick and mortar" closed down their shops to minimize their costs and soon realized that they had made a huge mistake; most of them

Exhibit 4.1   Consumer-Driven Key Retailing Trends

Trends	Causal Factors
E-tailing	More elderly than ever before, more computer ownership, more busy consumers who don't have time to shop
Wholesale discount places are multiplying	The relative income of the lower middle class has been stagnant; hence, they need good values
Discount department stores are emerging	Consumer's need for lower price and large varieties with more convenience than what wholesale discounters offer
Retail stores per 1,000 of population are increasing	The need for convenience as a countertrend of the need for low prices. Consumers want convenience products to be located nearby.
High-class retailing is maintaining its existence	The relative importance of the upper class has increased more than proportionately. They maintain their loyalty to high-class retailing facilities.
Franchising has continued to grow sharply	The need to be entrepreneurial and independent, while reducing risk by using already tried and successful retailing practices

failed. But "brick and mortar" retailers who added e-tailing capabilities have done rather well.

During the past three decades, American income distribution has become worse. While the upper one percent income has gone up substantially, middle-class incomes have been stagnant at best. The incomes of the lower income groups have gotten worse. As a result of these changes in the income distribution, the next four trends presented in Exhibit 4.1 emerged. Both discount wholesale and discount department stores have appealed more and more to the middle and lower middle classes with stagnating incomes. McDonaldization or commoditization in discounting products in fast food areas has become more and more common.

At the same time, either because consumers are working long, hard hours or because they are becoming more convenience prone, there seems to be an increase in the number of retail stores per 1,000 populations. Particularly, there has been an increase in convenience store numbers, such as small, local fast-food eating places and other necessary goods and services providing retail establishments.

The next trend in Exhibit 4.1 relates to resilience of high-class retailing. With the substantial increase in income of the upper income group in our society, high-class retailing has been getting a tremendous boost. Some of the very expensive upscale retailers are doing very well, and their future appears to be very bright. Their future depends on the continuation of the current income distribution in the American society.

Franchising is the next trend. Franchises are allowed to buy out part of a large well-known multiunit chain. Here, individual ownership is facilitated with somewhat reduced risk. However, franchising does not mean a full-fledged entrepreneurship since franchises are requested to follow certain patterns and dwell upon mostly standardized product lines and cooperative advertising. During the past three decades franchising arrangements in American retailing have increased substantially (Berman and Evans 2009). Franchising has also been a powerful driver of the global expansion of retailing. From fast food establishments to discount department stores, many international franchising arrangements have emerged in many parts of the world. It is critical to realize that most franchising arrangements provide some degree of freedom for individual units, such as adjusting their product mixes and localizing their appeals and services. To this extent, some 600,000 or more franchises of different types throughout the United States can benefit from many ideas that are presented throughout this book. The emergence of the Internet as a competing retailing alternative has also created a side trend in many "brick and mortar" retailers who wanted to compete better with e-tail offering something special to their customers. They started thinking of some entertainment or some other attraction for them so that they will find it to be fun to shop in these retail establishments.

ORGANIZATION TRENDS

The dynamic nature of the markets, with which the retailing sector interacts, forces retailing organization to make changes as well. In recent years, for instance, the number of retail establishments that are incorporated has been decreasing as a percent of total retail population. Part of this is due to mergers and acquisitions that are taking place in the sector. Similarly, small scale retailing has been increasing. The fact that the sales volume share of retailing corporations is perhaps at an all-time high, with a percentage share of around 90 percent of total retail sales, indicates that there is a high level of concentration power. That concentration of power indicates the fact that retail giants and discounters are very much in control. This makes it more difficult for small and medium-sized retailers to survive. Being there and being conveniently located does not mean these small independent institutions naturally survive. They have to be innovative enough to deliver a better quality of retailing service. This book attempts to identify some of the ways to accomplish that.

When the number of incorporated institutions is getting smaller but their share of total sales is getting larger, this situation implies that the merger and acquisition activity in the sector is continuing which is creating a concentration of economic power. This is combined with the fact that well-established upscale retailers are also doing well. An estimated 650,000 of them fail or disappear yearly. This is about the same number of those that enter the market every year. As retail giants and discounters offer one-stop shopping and discounted prices, most of the entrepreneurial independents are not even emphasizing offering, at least, convenience and personalized service which could be their strength. This is why almost 40 percent of all retail establishments have a declining share of total retailing volume (SBA 2012).

The era of independent medium to large-scale retailing, meaning independent department stores emphasizing self-service and catering to middle-class consumers appears to be somewhat gone since the share of department stores of total retailing has gone down (SBA 2012). This is partially due to the decline of the American middle class. Additionally, discounting has been pushing its competitive edge and luring department store customers. Thus, large department stores are being replaced by discount chains.

It is critical for a retailer to detect and understand trends in the society that are influencing the retailing sector. These trends, particularly for national retail chains, can be a threat, but they can also be great opportunities.

Recent Consumer Trends

American consumers have been experiencing certain forces that are modifying their lives. These modifications have direct and indirect impact on retailing. A major part of the consumer trends is related to the exploding cyberspace. Consumers and retailers have tremendously fast increasing information generated by electronic technology. Through hand-held devices consumers are capable of finding products in store, comparing prices, and determining on the availability of different brands and much more. Similarly, as discussed in different sections of this book, the retailer can directly communicate with customers in and out of store, detecting their behavior in and out of store and perhaps catering to their needs more carefully. Of course, this is the basic strategy of the retailers who cannot be cheaper than the discounters. Thus, consumers are more informed and more sensitive to what they buy and retailers must accommodate the needs of their customers to create *differential advantage*.

Developments impacting the consumer's lives have a very strong impact on the retailers' activities. Although consumers are working longer hours and making less money, there are also other trends. In general, consumers are getting married at a later date and having fewer children. There are also other trends. Furthermore, there are many divorces. Divorced people or single people have a little more money and consider spoiling themselves once in a while; as a result, there are a group of retail establishments categorized as new luxuries (Silverstein and Fiske 2005). Depending upon the location and the target market, the independent retailer will have to accommodate to these and other related trends. Thus, the question must be asked: how can I serve my customers better? Some of the trends impacting consumers directly may be in one one-stop shopping, in the area of product mix variety, and others may be related to discounting. But certainly, as discussed in many parts of this book, there is room for convenience, easy shopping, personal attention, particular product availability, and other features which can be implemented by the individual retailers who cannot be discount giants. Some six recent consumer trends are briefly discussed here.

Development of Electronic Communication

Perhaps the most profound trend during the past decade has been the development of electronic communication capabilities of consumers, which make the individual consumer able to obtain more information and negotiate with the retailer to compare prices and brands as they are shopping in or out of store. As discussed earlier, this situation is forcing the retailer to be both "bricker" and "clicker." But some very successful independent retailers have also learned to personalize their customers rather than treating them as a number. Making its customers feel they are important individuals is not something discounters will do but smaller independents can.

Changing Lifestyles

As socioeconomic conditions change, by definition, consumer's shopping habits also change. As indicated earlier, harder-working consumers who are making somewhat less money may need more convenience in shopping along with greater discounts. During the past decade or so, American consumers displayed a number of consumption trends, including the desire for low-fat and low-carb products, health foods and supplements, computer games, and home improvement supplies. This list could go on much longer. Naturally, detecting these trends early would give retailers "the first mover advantage." But, looking at the big picture, retailers who do not follow changing lifestyle trends and swiftly catering to these new trends do not do well in the market.

Consumer Demographics

American society is growing older. Baby boomers are becoming retirees. The older and faster growing segments have reasonable amounts of money and are going for more sporty cars, travel, and entertainment. Facilities for assisted living are expanding, along with the demand for pharmaceuticals and other health-care activities. Additionally, American society is becoming more multicultural, which leads to demand related to cultural values of immigrants. The independent retailer must be aware of changes that are taking place in their market.

Increasing Retail Competition

As mentioned previously, retail competition is increasing in favor of discounts. Consumers, to a large extent, are lured by one-stop shopping and discounting. However, there are those who opt for convenience and special personalization by retailers. Those independent retailers who cannot offer special service and proper convenience, among other features that are appreciated by modern consumers, are unfortunately disappearing, meaning that they are failing. Some 680,000 small businesses are not doing well. Most of them are small and medium-sized retailers (SBA Review 2012).

More e-Tailing

The attachment of the American consumer to hand-held electronic equipment provided the genesis of e-tailing. There are more consumers who like to play with this equipment which provided valuable information about product availability, market conditions, and similar types of information. e-Tailing is getting its impetus from the available and increasing information. The small and medium-sized retailers will have to use this trend to their advantage. Additionally, as mentioned earlier, the older consumer market is growing fast; it is reasonable to realize that this group, since some of their consumers are not very mobile and do not have the energy to shop physically, are more dependent on e-tailing.

International Retailers

During the past three decades or so, many developments in the direction of internationalization of American retailing have taken place. Not only foreign-owned retail establishments such as IKEA and Benetton flourished, but many non-American brands have also became popular. Simultaneously, many nonbranded items, particularly in the apparel sector, have been imported and branded in the Unites States for sale. Similarly, numerous American brands and retail establishments found their way into foreign markets. Names such as IBM, McDonalds, Walmart, and Apple among many others have established successful outreach operations. Certainly, these activities broadened the choice of American consumers around the world in terms of selection as well as price.

In exploring recent trends in the retail population, one must also analyze certain key economic factors that have impacted directly as well as indirectly on that population. However, it will be reasonable to state that international competition is not likely to impact the small and medium independent American retailers.

CRITICAL ECONOMIC TRENDS

Numerous critical trends have emerged, during the past three decades or so, in the overall economic setting within which the retailing sector functions. Among these are business cycles, changing economic profiles, and political environment.

Business Cycles

Small retailers, perhaps more than any other type of business, suffer from the impact of business cycles. On the average, as mentioned earlier, 680,000 businesses, most of whom are small retailers, exit the market. Most of these disappearances or failures are caused not so much by managerial missteps as by adversities in the economy. Along with an increase in the number of business failures, during recessions comes an increase in the number of small retailers. This is because many people who are laid off because of the recession try to establish their own businesses. But many of them are not properly prepared to own and run their stores; they fail in a short period of time. These failures are costly not only to individuals who are closely related to the failed entrepreneurs who started these businesses, but to the economy as well.

There are no guarantees for survival, but it is possible to develop a counter-business cycle strategy for these small and vulnerable retailers. Some of these countercyclical measures are discussed in different parts of this book. Suffice it to say here that in recessions small businesses must be able to adjust their retail mixes. Lower-priced product mixes with more classical and traditional lines, coupled with better service and increased promotion, are necessary ingredients of counter-recession strategies. At no time can small retailers afford to lower the services and quality they deliver by laying off employees or resorting to offer a poorer quality of merchandise; cutting costs by reducing promotional expenses or charging more for products and services have proven success. In fact, these actions have been deadly particular during recession periods. All of the practices to reduce value and charge more, which is the unfortunate tendency on the part of small retailers during recession periods, would prove to be detrimental for the individual establishments.

Changing Consumer Profiles

As mentioned earlier, income distribution in the United States has been changing in a dramatic manner in favor of the upper fifth and particularly, top 1 percent of the population (Samli 2013). Thus, economic wellbeing of the middle class has been frozen while the lower economic class has been deteriorating further. As a result, department stores appealing to the middle class are having a very difficult time. Discounters and fast food chains, low-priced retailers such as category killers, and large-scale wholesale operations dealing in retailing such as Costco have been doing well.

Another aspect of changing consumer profiles is the changing combination of the total population. Increased ethnic minorities are becoming rather powerful and are exerting their cultural preferences in product and service mixes.

Political Environment

Although strictly speaking not an economic factor, the political environment is playing a critical role in the retailing sector, along with the economy as a whole. Permissive merger-mania tendencies have not been discouraged. As a result, many companies are merging. Merger mania is not necessarily increasing competition. It is, rather, the opposite; it is reducing competition in favor of retail giants (Samli 2013). Similarly, outsourcing has not been discouraged and as a result, discounters have been getting dramatically lower-priced products from China, India, and other third-world countries. Once again, this is benefiting the discounters and partially the consumers. But it is not having a positive impact on small and medium-sized independent retailers. Similarly, availability of credit and lending activities of the financial sector has not been in favor of small independents. The financial sector has favored retail giants rather than small independents.

There are many other considerations that primarily belong in economics books. But, it is important to reiterate that retailers, particularly small-scale retailers, are influenced by many trends in the economy such as the local economy. These trends may help or hinder the activities of these independents. It is, therefore, critical for a retailer to spot these trends, understand their implications, and use them to their advantage if possible. Survival for a retailer, in a sense, is the manipulation of probabilities. The higher the probability of success, the better off the retail establishment.

Managing the trends influencing the survival of the retail establishment is a must. Small-scale retailing always faces a greater risk than large-scale retail establishments and chains. This is because the small-scale establishments do not have large financial resources on which to rely on in times of hardship. Hence, small retailers need to pay attention to trends, particularly the trickle effect of national trends on the local economy. Additionally, local development which may not be part of national trends can be particularly important for small independents. A local-scale construction or a major highway development can have very strong direct impact on these small retailers. It is not an exaggeration to state that the small retailer needs to be a particular combination of sociologist, economist, and political scientist in addition to being a competent retailer.

THE "E" REVOLUTION

Although it is touched upon throughout the book, it is extremely important to consider the "E" revolution that has been going on for over a decade now. It is a major trend in communication which is profound by influencing the retailing sector. By enhancing data generation, data storage, and data transmission, information technology (IT) enhanced the emergence of more efficiently functioning retailing sectors. Improved local, national, and global communication has been and is creating tremendous benefits to consumers and challenges retailers (Strauss, El-Ansary, and Frost 2006). IT, as a part of total information system (IS), is used readily by national and international retailing giants for competitive purposes, but it must be very strongly stated that small retailers will have to be very efficient in using IT to communicate with their customers. Both IT and IS provide very important advantages over the traditional retailing. The retailing giants are locked in competition with one another and, hence, any cost cutting and decision-making tools that IT provides are not only beneficial, but necessary.

As already implied, small and medium-sized retailers must use IT more than the giants if they want to be better and survive. But, they must learn to use IT not because they are competing with the retail giants, but because they are creating better shopping conditions for their customers. IT and IS enable small retailers to customize their merchandise mixes and their service offerings. However, this means a better utilization of IT and IS by small retailers to move from mass retailing to relationship retailing (Strauss, El-Ansary, and Frost 2006). Exhibit 4.2 illustrates the contrast between large-scale retailing and small-scale retailing in the utilization of IT and IS. While the large-scale retailing concentrates on one sale at a time, the small-scale retailer must think of continuity. By definition, large-scale retailing has a short-term orientation; small-scale retailing must emphasize the long term.

The large-scale retailing emphasizes one-way communication through advertising and small-scale retailing would gain an advantage by creating two-way communication. While the large-scale retailing focuses immediate sales, and have the approach of come and get it, small-scale retailing must create a relationship focus. That proper behavior is roughly touched upon by the points made in Exhibit 4.2.

Exhibit 4.2 Contrast between Large-Scale versus Small-Scale Retailing

Large-Scale Retailing	Small-Scale Retailing
Discrete transactions	Continuing transactions
Short-term orientation	Long-term emphasis
One-way communication	Two-way communication
Sales focus	Relationship focus
Market share	Customer satisfaction
Marketing strategy emphasis	Customer relationship emphasis

Source: Adapted and revised from Strauss, El-Ansary and Frost (2006).

The contrast described in that exhibit is the general description of what independent small retailers might do for success. The large-scale retailers are typically preoccupied with their share of the market while small-scale retailers can gain an advantage only by emphasizing customer satisfaction. Finally, the large-scale retailers emphasize marketing strategy while small-scale retailers must emphasize customer relationship. But it is questionable if small-scale retailers can use the IT and IS in the way it is described here. Clearly the two groups have different orientations in using IT and IS.

One of the ways the small-scale retailers may use IT successfully is by using Radio Frequency Identification (RFID), which was developed in early 2000 (Supermarket Guru 2003). This process can develop a better customer relationship on an individualized basis.

Summary

It is critical for a retailer to detect trends in society. Although these trends can be a threat, they can also be a great opportunity. The trends that are cited in this chapter have been particularly critical for retailing. It is clear that small-scale retailers must be able to detect these trends and understand their impact on their businesses. The message to small-scale retailers is that: *you must do a better job in creating customer value*. Creating of customer value begins with understanding customer trends. But understanding the trends is not enough; they must be managed properly. In other words, small-scale retailing thrives on steady and loyal customers; therefore, long-term relationship with customers is critical. Following the come and get it approaches, large-scale retailers have one way of communication leading to sales in the short run. The small-scale retailer has to have a two-way communication to continue its long-term emphasis. Similarly, the large-scale retailer is selling right there and receiving immediate sales results, again, the small-scale retailer is counting on long-term relationship connection with its customers.

5

THE RETAIL EVOLUTION

If we don't know how we got here, it will be hard to decide the best way to go next. Not knowing the natures of the evolution which took place in the retail sector of this country makes it almost impossible for a new retailer to function. Just what may be expected to be the far-reaching impact of developments in retailing? How these changes are likely to touch our particular business must be a constant concern on which to ponder. Although selectively, revolutionary changes take place, retailing typically experienced a continuing evolution.

Retailing takes place in specific places and in specific forms according to population movements and resultant population concentration areas. It must be reiterated that in our market economy, unless they generate consumer value, retail establishments cannot survive. The fact that some 680,000 small businesses, most of which are retailers, are going out of existence indicates that they were not able to generate consumer value. While consumer value is created by price, variety and one-stop shopping are created by retail giants. Small-scale retailers will have to emphasize convenience, ease of shopping, and additional services. If consumers can find proper products and services without traveling long distances, with the help and advice of friendly retail personnel the small-scale retailers are establishing some market power, which will enhance their survival opportunities and their profit pictures.

The retailing sector has been generating consumer value in three distinct ways simultaneously; by being accessible, by providing the necessary goods and services, and by grouping with other retailers that complement the total offering. But, with the major population movements from rural to urban and from urban to suburban, retailing also made certain critical adjustments. In the rural era retailing facilities were not plentiful and not conveniently located. In urban settings at the very beginning only downtowns or central business districts (CBDs) offered the necessary goods and services, they were not very convenient. In suburban development retailing primarily relied on shopping centers and shopping malls. As traffic got heavier, people spent more time at work, and petroleum became more expensive, preference for convenience increased. This is where the small scale independents are likely to be benefited by serving local consumers well.

KEY EVOLUTIONARY AREAS

Basically, American population has been and is very mobile. As it moved from urban to suburban settings, the emphasis became more concentrated on one-stop shopping and primarily on self-service. Leaving consumers alone to do their shopping in an organized store atmosphere was the general orientation of department stores. These department stores became the focal points in shopping centers. Retailing, being close and catering to suburbia, became quite successful. Large department store chains such as Sears did well. Downtowns responded with specialized small, elegant boutiques and specialty stores that make consumers come back to downtowns and make their shopping experiences exciting and colorful.

As the population became more and more dispersed, retailing also became dispersed, with convenience stores, ice cream parlors, small pizzerias, and video stores, to name but a few types of shops. Retailing while trying to reach out and stay in close proximity to the population, also tried to attract people from other towns, communities, and other population centers. If and when consumers are not satisfied with the existing retailing facilities in their town, and very attractive retail facilities have emerged in neighboring areas, consumers did out-shopping.

Out-shopping

As population became more and more dispersed, many relatively isolated small towns, somewhat isolated communities, dormitory communities, where people live but work and shop elsewhere, became rather common. This created the concept of out-shopping or an intermarket shopping phenomenon. This is an important concept that all small and medium-sized independent retailers must understand. As people go out of the area where they live to shop, there may be some intermarket shopping patterns. These could be very important for retailers who can detect and work with these patterns. As populations became more mobile and as communications about shopping opportunities for consumers became more available, intermarket mobility for retailing purposes has become rather powerful.

A Model for Intermarket Shopping

Exhibit 5.1 presents a model of intermarket purchase behavior. It indicates why people may go out of town to shop. The model revolves around the needs and wants of consumers. It points of, in a very general sense, how these needs and wants emerge and how they are taken care of. Consumers' needs and wants are generated, stimulated, and modified by their lifestyles. Lifestyles, in turn, are formed by the consumer's level of education and their degree of sophistication. Their general background is also a part of this equation and, certainly, related to their degree of sophistication. If a consumer has refined needs and wants that local retailing facilities cannot accommodate, then consumers are likely to out-shop. Where they go is partially based on their loyalty to the town or the area where they live, as well as on the attractiveness of other shopping facilities in other towns or cities. However, distance is always a deterrent, which can be partially overcome by strong promotional activity from other shopping centers. If the promotional activity is strong enough, consumers may ignore the problem of distance. Thus, some consumers from southwest Virginia may fly out to the DC area or to New York occasionally for shopping because these shopping facilities are extensively advertised and offer tremendous varieties of products and services as well as certain types of entertainment.

Exhibit 5.1 A General Model of Intermarket Purchase Behavior

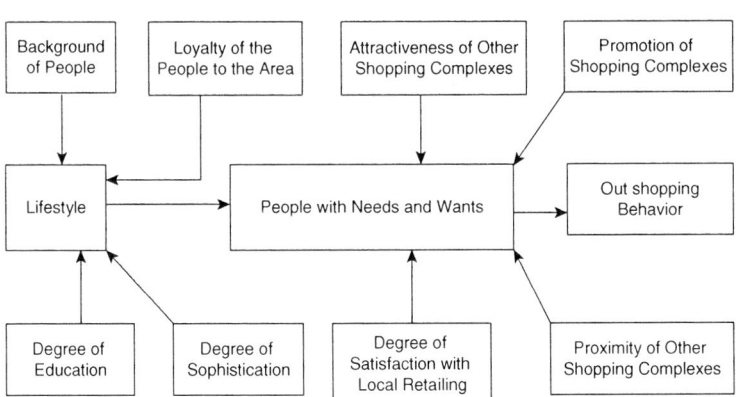

For small communities with retailers who are not sensitive enough or do not understand the needs of consumers and their behavior patterns, intermarket purchasing of this type could be borderline devastating. Small communities experiencing lots of out shopping cannot generate enough income to develop their retailing facilities further, and they remain dormant.

In recent years, intermarket shopping behavior has become particularly critical, for instance, when Walmart and a few other giants start an attractive and rather modern shopping center out of town or out of the area. In such cases the regular independent retailers of the area must establish very close relationship with their customers so that they can improve the services they offer, make it easier and comfortable to shop at and improve their merchandise mixes much more to the liking of their regular customers along with more acceptable pricing practices.

From Downtown to Shopping Centers

During the final three decades of the twentieth century, the retail evolution took a very powerful move from well-established and older downtowns to suburban and regional shopping centers. Emerging shopping centers encouraged out shopping and took consumers away from downtowns, also called CBDs. CBDs during this time appeared to be suffering from lack of vision and competitive creativity. Many downtown stores had been there for a long period of time and have done the same things year in and year out. Therefore, they were suffering from an acute case of inertia. During that era and some cases even today downtowns have been under pressure to do something to reverse their declining profitability and appeal.

Five specific reasons—population dispersion, uncoordinated marketing, emergence of shopping centers, decreasing accessibility and inertia—may explain the flight of downtowns.

Population Dispersion

About one-fifth of the American population moves every year. In such a dynamic society it is natural to expect major trends in population movement. Among these are exoduses from the Northeast to the Southwest and from the Midwest to the Southeast. But perhaps the most important population movement has been from cities to suburbs. Thus, the population is not only mobile, but dispersing as well. As markets are dispersing, it is becoming difficult for the retailer to keep abreast of the population movement patterns and to satisfy changing consumer needs. Such movements have particularly been adversely affecting downtown retailing complexes.

Uncoordinated Marketing

Downtown retailing complexes are typically composed of many independent entrepreneurs, who own their stores and run their businesses independently. This is one of the key problems of CBDs. Downtowns need not only modernization but also coordinated marketing and merchandising efforts, downtown establishments traditionally are varied and individualistic without any identified and implemented patterns. Thus, the promotional efforts traditionally have not been coordinated, and thus, typically, downtowns do not have a clear-cut and appealing identity. Thus, CBDs not only have lacked synergism but also have moved rather aimlessly. For instance, coordinated special sales, advertising, or other special effects, which could bring about a synergistic impact, have been rarely experienced in downtown activities.

Emerging Shopping Centers

During the past half century or so, retailing's response to population dispersion has been the emergence of shopping centers that provided a large variety of products and one-stop shopping along with parking. These shopping centers were planned in terms of appeal, offering, and promotion. They were the antithesis of CBDs. They emerged as American suburbia mushroomed. This retailing phenomenon first came into existence in the early 1950s. Unlike downtowns, shopping centers displayed five important features that made them successful. First, these shopping complexes are very accessible for the consumers who were tired of crowded downtowns and traffic snags that made it difficult to shop. Second, they were modern well-planned facilities that provide extensive one-stop shopping for more mobile and discriminating consumers who lived in suburbia or even came from downtowns. Third, parking was made simple and easy. All shopping centers were, and are, surrounded by adequate parking facilities that cannot be compared to the crowded conditions of downtown shopping complexes. Fourth, they pursued coordinated merchandising and marketing activities of the whole complex. Fifth, and finally, shopping centers presented general themes and architecture sometimes reflecting certain cultural orientation, which made them unique and attractive.

Decreasing Accessibility

As the car population increased on the existing highways, the roads did not increase and improve proportionately; as a result downtown traffic became difficult to cope with. Naturally, access to shopping became progressively worse. This is partly why people fled from downtowns to shopping centers and suburbia.

Inertia

The type of inertia that is particularly related to the practices of retailers in downtowns had been going on for a long time. Many of the downtown retailers did not know how to change and improve their business practices. As market conditions became adverse, many of them did not have the capability to cope with emerging problems. As a result many of them failed.

As a result of these five negative factors, downtowns throughout the country became thoroughly challenged and also in trouble. But after some 60 years shopping centers are becoming old and some efforts are taking place to revive downtowns. However, this is a rather complicated problem; most people who are in charge of downtown revival do not quite have good ideas to accomplish that. But a few have been rather successful in developing attractive downtowns which would appeal to some of the suburbanites as well as tourists. New and successful downtowns have entertainment, boutiques, museums and good restaurants. This certainly requires a major planning and coordination activity.

FROM MALLS TO LOCAL CLUSTERS

As shopping centers emerged, they also started competing with one another. One of the most logical ways of competing was controlling atmospheres. This led to the emergence of enclosed shopping malls. In time, malls also started competing among themselves in terms of overall appeal, merchandise mix, quality, and service as well as through other promotional activities such as concerts and displays and the like. Most of the malls are large and somewhat equal to regional shopping centers. But as population continued dispersing further from within and without suburbia, as transportation became more expensive and aging became a reality, it became necessary to have shopping facilities more conveniently located for local consumers. Consequently, there emerged three new retailing complexes: community shopping centers, neighborhood shopping complexes, and neighborhood clusters.

Community shopping centers: They are located in about 15–20 minutes driving time. They typically have 15–50 stores. They have moderate assortments of shopping goods and convenience products. Principally in these complexes are discount department stores or one major department store-based complexes. They are typically L-shaped. They are reasonably well planned with their overall activities and about 15 offerings.

Neighborhood shopping complexes: These facilities are located around 5–10 minutes driving time; they usually have 10–15 stores. They typically cluster around a supermarket or a major drugstore. They are strip shaped. They offer a limited assortment of shopping goods and other convenience products. They are not well planned.

Neighborhood clusters: These are groups of stores in residential areas. They are within three to five minutes of walking distance. They usually have less than ten stores. Their total emphasis is on convenience. They do not have a principal store. Most of the stores in these complexes are convenience oriented such as a bakery, an ice cream parlor, a barbershop, a sandwich shop and the like. These complexes are not planned they thrive on the basis of their evaluation of the local market potential (Samli 2004).

In all three groups of retail facilities independent small or medium-sized retailers are very, very much in the present. Thus, a small retailer, for instance, must observe the characteristic of the retailing complex it is in and how the complex is performing. By doing so that individual retailer could improve its own performance and can make a better contribution to the overall performance of the complex.

FROM BRICKS TO CLICKS

In recent years, retail evolution has taken the industry to a higher plateau, which is e-tailing. Some consumers do not like to shop around while some others are insufficiently mobile. In both cases they can buy almost anything they wish to buy anywhere in the world by using the Internet. The emergence of e-trade or e-tail activity came along somewhat suddenly and created a shock in the retailing sector. Many retailers treated cyberspace as a total market with its own demand and supply, and with its own communication and delivery systems. These retailers went completely away from "bricks" to "clicks". They closed down their businesses and went exclusively on line. This was not the best alternative. Most of the exclusive clickers did not survive.

A second alternative was to treat cyberspace as a distribution channel. Most retailers reduced their regular bricking activities in favor of clicking. Once again, this did not enhance their retailing position. They could not promote sales and deliver merchandise and hence many ceased to exist.

The third alternative was to treat cyberspace as a communication channel, a supplement to existing communication activity. These retailers simply added the Internet to their communication mix. Unlike the first two groups above, this third group has done and is still doing quite well. Almost all of the well-known names in retailing have developed their Internet capabilities and are using e-trading as an extension of their regular activities. They communicate with customers on line; they receive orders on line that are to be picked up at their brick and mortar complexes, thus improving communications and reducing waiting time for delivery. Being a well-known bricker and adding clicking capabilities, at this point in time, appears to be a very positive development in the never ending retail evolution. Thus, the last part of this evolutionary movement has been going back to bricks but not ignoring clicks. It has been said that today's customers demand accessibility to their favorite brands across multiple channels. Customers still like to touch and experience a product before they buy it. But they appreciate more and advanced information. This is why online and brick-and-mortar combinations will continue (Conor 2014).

However, particularly small retailers are rather behind on their e-trade capabilities. As discussed in different sections of this book, coping with retail giants necessitates proficiency and capability in utilizing modern computer-generated information and e-trade capabilities.

The Discounting Era

Particularly when economic conditions are not very bright, discount retailing becomes particularly popular. During the past three decades or so, discounters such as Walmart, Target, Costco, and others have become very popular and powerful. They seem to be replacing conventional shopping centers with the same promise of great selection and one-stop shopping but additional discounted pricing. As mentioned earlier, this may be called the era of discounting. What is important here is that although old department stores had discount basements only people with limited income shopped there. However, the modern discount giants are attracting customers from all walks of life. These discount giants do not particularly offer customer services, and do not pay particular attention to individuals, they have very large number of customers, and they mostly treat them as numbers. This is one of the key points the small- and medium-scale independent retailers may take advantage of. They cannot beat discounters' prices but certainly they could offer more and better services.

It must be stated that discount giants prefer stand-alone stores to malls (Raghavendra 2014). Although this may have cost advantages, independent retailers as part of an attractive cluster may be more appealing to consumers.

SUMMARY

This chapter dealt with some of the most important aspects of American retail evolution. Among these trends are: from downtown to shopping centers, population dispersion, from malls to local clusters, from bricks to clicks, and the discounting era. It must be stated that these evolutionary movements are still in action. The critical point here is that small- and medium-scale independent retailers must know the danger and benefit of these movements and act accordingly.

Additionally, the chapter discussed an out-shopping phenomenon which still goes on forcefully.

6

Capitalizing on Market Potentials

Throughout this book, the location theme has been repeated. Retailing not only follows the population dispersion, but also locates conveniently to certain population groups. It must be stressed forcefully that location is the first life bloods of retailing. No matter how good, how attractive, or how accommodating, if a retailer is not located properly, there is no possibility that it can achieve success.

If the macro- and microeconomic conditions are favorable, then the retailer should go ahead and start the business. But, it must be remembered that approximately 30 percent of new retail establishments survive less than six months. At least three primary activities should be conducted to indicate that both macro- and microconditions are all favorable for the proposed retail establishment to start. Here, the macroeconomic conditions indicate that it is a growing community; the average income is reasonable and there is no widespread unemployment problem. The microconditions indicate that the approximate location is good and there are reasonably appropriate retail facilities in the close proximity.

The three preliminary activities proposed here are the following: assessing market potentials, evaluating the feasibility of the proposed retail establishment, and determining the capital needs of the proposed store. All three of these activities must precede the preopening activities that are discussed in chapter 1.

Geographic Dimensions and Market Potentials

Retail location is not a very flexible activity such as advertising or pricing; once the store is located it cannot be changed. Thus, it is important to connect the proposed location to market potentials before the location decision is carefully studied and finalized. This decision must be made carefully and in advance of everything.

Preliminary location analysis must guide the retailer to be in the direction of making concrete location decisions. These preliminary analyses must include: (1) choosing the approximate location, (2) assessing the area's growth and its actual potential, and (3) evaluating that area's *retail saturation level*.

Unlike major retail chains, independent retailers to be are not likely to choose the most dynamic location in which to locate its store. In other words, small independents may not have the skills or options to undertake objective analysis of location options. Typically, an independent retailer to be goes with familiarity rather than solid economic criteria for the first line of decisions, choosing approximately where to locate.

All national chains such as *International House of Pancakes*, *Kroger*, and *CVS* employ formulas regarding the opening of a new unit in their chain. Unless the conditions in the formula are satisfied, they will not open a new unit in a new location. These conditions include such items as economic growth, base population, competition, and the like. Thus, the location decisions for major national or international retailers are rather scientific and are designed to reduce risk and enhance profitability.

An independent retailer to be faces a different problem. The chances are that the general area where the store may be located is likely to be based, somewhat arbitrarily, on the familiarity of that retailer to be. However, even though it may not be common practice, that does not mean the choice of approximate location should go through a careful and very detailed analysis.

Exhibit 6.1 illustrates a seven-step complete plan for general analysis before the proposed store becomes a real entity. The steps in the exhibit start with the identification of the general area where the proposed retail establishment is likely to be located.

The second step in Exhibit 6.1 is delimiting the trading area where the expected customers of the proposed store are likely to come from. The particular area where the proposed retail establishment is likely to be located and what is that area's retailing potential are very critical considerations. This area may be a whole town or a neighboring town and the like. To take care of these two steps, many different techniques may be used. Here, four different approaches are briefly discussed. These techniques are: buying power index (BPI), percentage of expenditures, special bottom-up, and geographic information system (GPS).

Exhibit 6.1   Assessing Marketing Potentials and Capital Needs

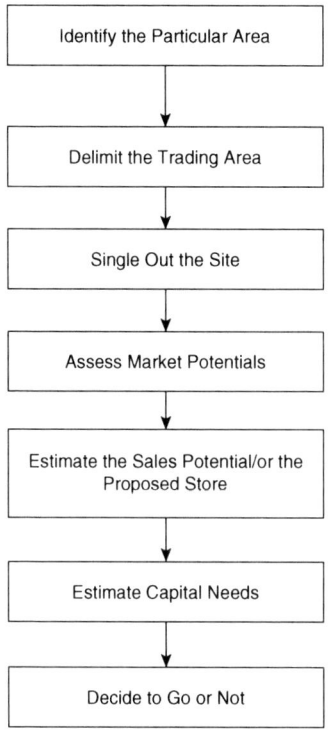

Exhibits 6.2–6.5 deal with these four approaches respectively. Exhibit 6.2 illustrates the sales and marketing management BPI approach. *Sales and Marketing Management Journal* has been presenting a BPI for more than five decades. Even though it discontinued constructing this technique, it is an important approach and can be calculated individually. Originally, this instrument was composed of three key variables that are representing a region or a town. These are total income, total sales, and total population. Originally, these three variables were assigned three separate weights: 5, 3, and 2 respectively. As can be seen in the exhibit, assuming a town's percent share of national total in the exhibit are 1.1, 0.4, and 0.5 respectively. With the weights used as multipliers, the total becomes 7.7 divided 10 equals 0.77. This means that 0.77 is the total sales volume approximated of the national total. That would be the BPI of that community. If the national sales of, say, automobiles is 10 million, 0.77 percent of that would be the approximate share of the community in question. Again, if the national

Exhibit 6.2   The Use of Buying Power Index[a]

Income[b]	1.1% × 5 = 5.5
Retail Sales[c]	0.4% × 3 = 1.2
Population[d]	0.5% × 2 = 1.0
	7.7 ÷ 10 = 0.77

[a] Hypothetical figures.
[b] Income as a percentage of national total.
[c] Retail sales as a percentage of national total.
[d] Population as a percentage of national total.

Exhibit 6.3   District of Jacksonville, Florida and National Distribution of Expenditures of Food

Income Per Household	Percentage of All Households	Total Percentage of Expenditures on Food in US
$10,000–14,999	5.2	23.9
$15,000–24,999	12.1	21.0
$50,000 and over	44.0	8.0

Note: Hypothetical number of households 425,525.
Source: Dept. of Commerce, Dept. of Labor (hypothetical figures).

Exhibit 6.4   Estimated Total Personal Income, Number of Households in Each Income Category and Expenditures on Food, Jacksonville, Florida

Income Per Household	Number of Units[a]	Total Estimated Income[b]	Total Estimated Expenditures[c] of Food
$10,000–14,999	22,127	276,591,200.00	65,105,309.00
$15,000–24,999	51,409	1,029,770,500.00	216,251,805.00
$25,000–49,999	133,189	4,994,599,687.00	329,427,566.00
$50,000 and over	187,231	17,786,645,000.00	1,422,955,600.00

[a] Estimates are based on household percentages in Exhibit 6-3 multiplied by the total number of households (Hypothetical).
[b] Number of households are multiplied by the midpoint of income per household, with the exception of the last category, in which an annual average income of $90,000 is utilized.
[c] Total income figures are multiplied by the total percentage of expenditure figures in Exhibit 6-3.

auto tires sale is $2 billion, 0.77 percent will be the estimated sales volume for the community in question. In calculation, 7.7 is divided by 10 since the total weight of the three variables is 10.

Exhibits 6.3 and 6.4 display total expenditures in a specified area for a specific product line. By calculating total incomes of different

Exhibit 6.5   Estimating Market Potential for a Service Station

Steps
1. Number of automobiles in the specific area = 50,000
2. Number of service stations in the specified area = 50
3. Average number of cars per service station

$$\frac{\text{Number of autos}}{\text{Number of service stations}} = \frac{50,000}{50} = 1,000 \text{ cars per station}$$

4. Cost associated with car maintenance and operation (including gas, oil, and service)
   Cost of driving one mile = $0.55
   Average mileage driven per year = 12,000
   Cost of driving one mile × average mileage drive per year 0.55 × 12.000 = $6.600
   per car including services
5. Cost per car times average number of cars per gas station 6,600 × 1,000 = $6,600.000
   on the average $6.6 million volume per service station

Note: Numbers change often and must be updated for accuracy.

income categories and connecting them to national average expenditures in each income category for that product category, it becomes possible to determine how much will be spent on the product category in question in that particular area. This is a top-down approach. It is utilized often, particularly by larger retailers. It is a macro-approach that can give a more general evaluation of market opportunities. Although the data in Exhibit 6.3 are hypothetical, the factual information needed can be obtained from the US Department of Commerce and the US Department of Labor. By, say, using the midpoints of income numbers and multiplying them by the number of households in that income category and calculating the percentage of expenditures on a commodity like milk, the total milk consumption can be calculated from the data presented in Exhibit 5.3. This approach is more readily illustrated in Exhibit 6.4. Again, from the percentages as shown in Exhibit 6.3, the number of units in each income category is calculated. And again, by using the percentage of total income spent, say, on food it becomes possible to calculate how much money each income category spends on food.

A special bottom-up approach is displayed in Exhibit 6.5. Unlike the previous two exhibits, this is strictly micro-approach. Small retailers are more in need of such creative micro-approaches. This is because small retailers are more closely bound by a specific location, and the overall market conditions are not the same at all sites. Such an approach displayed in Exhibit 6.5 can be used more readily for certain circumstances depending upon what is available and what is needed. In Exhibit 6.5, the market potential is derived from the number of automobiles. In another circumstance the number of cars per thousand people nationally, or the number of homes, or the number of people who live in the study area and many others may be used to establish market potential. It is partially dependent upon the retailer's imagination and knowledge.

In recent years, sophisticated computerization data systems have become available and can easily be used for location decisions. The GIS is one such example. This system is very versatile. It is a more expanded version of the percentages of expenditures approach. It can give the demographics of specific areas and can combine the demographics with expenditures on a variety of products and services. All of these approaches help to identify retailing opportunities.

EXPANDING TRADING AREAS

As has been mentioned in earlier chapters, with the advancement of the e-revolution it has clearly expanded the traditional concept of trading area. Consumers from adjacent communities know more about, say, our establishment and they can be engaged in intermarket purchase behavior directly or through the Internet.

As mentioned in my earlier book (Samli 2004), it is critical to at least approximately delineate the geographic area where the retail establishment is likely to draw customers. This delineated geographic area is called the retail trading area. Ideally, the identification of the trading area would be the cost of contact between the retailer and prospective customers. But, it also would enhance the effectiveness of any promotional activity to lure the prospective customers.

Geographic delineation of an area containing potential customers for a prospective retailer or a retailing complex such as a shopping center is critical. Only by such delineation can the feasibility of the proposed retail establishment or the retailing complex be established. This delineated geographic area, which is the retail trading area, is where the retailer has the greatest access to the market with the most potential. This also means that the same retailer will be able to create the most value for its customers.

The identification of the retail trading area is based on the following four steps:

1. Is there a critical mass of population that is likely to be patronizing the proposed retailing facility?

2. What is the proportion of the proposed critical mass that lives in the immediate area? For example, if 55–70 percent of the prospective customers live in the area, they will be identified as the primary trading area. If 15–25 percent of the prospective customers are located in the area, they may be identified as the secondary trading area. The remaining of the market may be identified as the fringe trading area.
3. What is the proportion of the purchases that will take place in the proposed retailing facility? Just what is the proposed retailing facility's competitive advantage?
4. Is there a way to determine from how far a distance some customers may come and what is the population concentration in those areas? And why they may be expected to come to the proposed retailing facility?

These four points must be operationalized so that the proposed retailing facility can decide how much and where it will put emphasis on promoting the new facility. However, additional information regarding (1) the demographic and socioeconomic characteristics of the prospective customers in the area, (2) the estimated future growth or decline potential of the area, and (3) the number of stores that the area can possibly support without becoming overcrowded by retail stores must also be calculated.

Obviously, a prospective new store's trading area is not based on current patronage patterns of the people, but on some evaluation of existing market potential (Samli 2004) of the proposed location and its outreach. As stated earlier, an approximation of the proposed stores trading area is based on the people who live in the geographic core from which the store would obtain its 55–70 percent of its business. This is followed by the secondary trading area from which the store gets 15–25 percent of its business. The fringe trading area and intermarket shoppers are considered to be simply additions but not to be counted on.

It may be reiterated that proximity is typically construed as the trading area's determining factor, which may be expressed in terms of distance and time (both in terms of driving and walking time). Here, the objective criteria of the number of people or the number of households in certain proximity, with the average income and proportion of spending on the type of business (e.g., groceries, apparel, etc.), would give the first line of estimations. It must be understood that this first line of estimations is a joint product of census tracts that give information that is related to housing units, number of people, income, education, and other basic information, and the Bureau of Labor statistics. The latter gives information regarding what proportion of income is spent on which general product and service categories by different income groups. By combining census tract data and Bureau of Labor statistics, estimates can be generated about the market potential in the geographic area. This is deemed as part of the trading area expressed in census tracts (Exhibit 6.4).

The objective criteria must be supplemented by some approximation of intermarket shopping tendencies. These approximations, among others, are based on surveys, traveling distance, and Internet, or e-trade involvement and observational efforts.

Surveys

Using survey techniques to determine the extent to which individuals are typically inclined to buying in the area versus going out of the area (intermarket shopping) is not new. In such attempts, determining the tendency for intermarket shopping indirectly is important. Instead of asking prospective customers if they will go to areas X, Y, Z to shop, it is better to find out where, when, and how much they have purchased of the product or the service categories in question. Needless to say, the information obtained by some survey techniques is not likely totally conclusive, but would indicate a tendency which could be important for an existing or a proposed retailing establishment.

Traveling Distance

The time spent to get to the retailing facility in question modified or strengthened by attractiveness of that facility plus relative lack of attractive facility in the home front could be strong factors leading to intermarket shopping. In other words, how much drawing power, if any, the proposed retail facility might have is a critical question and must be explored. The retailer will have to explore where and how much intermarket shopping tendencies may exist. If there is a specific area or two that appear to be possibilities, then there may be promotional efforts on the part of the retailer to attract potential customers.

E-Trade or the Internet Involvement

For the shopper who prefers to use the computer for shopping activity, the trading area is the whole world. In other words, he/she can buy virtually anything from anywhere in the world. Although e-trading has expanded substantially during the past decade, its total sales are estimated to be only around 5 percent of the total national retail sales. However, that is still a large volume, and a retailer, any retailer, must make an attempt to develop online sales. It is quite possible that there may be older people who would need special services such as home delivery of the products ordered online. Some independent retailers may consider this to be an area where they can do better than the giants.

Observation Efforts

Although it has been around long time, observation is not quite well utilized. Consider, for instance, a small retail cluster; the drawing power of that group of retailers, just where their customers are coming from, can be examined by analyzing the license plates of the cars that are driven by their customers. Each car's location is identified. Thus, it is possible to tell that the cluster in question is drawing mostly from the county A as opposed to B and C. Then the group could decide how they should promote the cluster (Samli 1996).

Thus far we have tried to identify and evaluate the trading area. But it must be realized that trading areas are not homogeneous and the impact of competition varies in different parts of trading areas. It is reasonable to generalize that for smaller independent retailers convenience and accessibility are critical. In such cases consumers who are closer to the retailing complex may frequent it more often. However, if there are other shopping opportunities they could easily be tempted to frequent them also. But perhaps, above all, within a trading area there are multiple possibilities for a retailing site.

SINGLING OUT THE SITE

Concerning the location of a proposed retail facility, be it a single store or a complex of stores such as a shopping center, it is essential there be multiple choices to choose from. If there is only one choice, the anxious retailer to be may become too uncritical of that available location and may overlook the shortcomings of the proposed site. This kind of bias could prove to be detrimental later on.

Assuming that there are four possible sites in the general trading area under scrutiny, it is necessary to develop a checklist and analyze each site accordingly. Exhibit 6.6 is developed for that purpose. As can be seen four possible sites are evaluated on the basis of 16 criteria. Certainly the number and nature of the criteria used could vary on the

Exhibit 6.6   Site Evaluation Checklist

Features	Site 1	Site 2	Site 3	Site 4
Traffic congestion (vehicular)	1	4	6	8
Highways connecting to the site	4	3	8	5
Adequacy of exits	1	2	3	2
Adequacy of parking	1	5	4	8
Attractiveness to pedestrians	4	4	8	6
Pedestrian safety	4	6	7	5
Density of pedestrian traffic	3	3	6	7
Landlords are cooperative	1	2	5	2
Maintenance of the facility	2	2	4	8
Availability of long-term leases	2	2	3	7
Rents are expected to be stable	1	2	2	3
Low level of absentee ownership	1	1	1	2
Economic and business activity is promising	2	4	5	7
Competition is not overwhelming	2	4	2	7
Proximity to other supportive retailing	1	4	3	8
Residents in the area are a good target	1	3	4	3
TOTAL	31	51	71	88

basis of unique conditions or on the preferences of the management of the proposed retailing concern. In the exhibit each site is evaluated by the total scores of the 16 criteria. The scoring used here has been 1 for the best-case scenario and 10 for the worst-case scenario. It is clear that site 1 is by far the best. It must be specified that in this evaluation exercise equal weight is given to all 16 variables. In certain circumstances the weights given to the variable could be different and a weighted average may have to be calculated to have the most meaningful choice. Despite the 16 specific variables identified in Exhibit 6.6, a proposed site may need to be analyzed in more general terms but in greater detail. Among others, in such cases most typical analysis may concentrate on traffic, history, accessibility, and legal aspects.

Traffic and History

Throughout this book, it is reiterated that traffic is the lifeblood of retailing. If a site is in a mall or a shopping center, then pedestrian traffic must be explored. On the other hand, if a location is considered for a new shopping center, a sole-standing super-discounter, or a cluster, then it is necessary to analyze the vehicular traffic along with pedestrian traffic counts. This type of information is usually considered along with national or regional statistics of the required traffic for possible success. If such data are not readily available, it may be necessary to develop a criterion by comparing the traffic of the proposed site with the traffic of a comparable retail complex that is known to be successful.

In analyzing the history of the proposed site, it is important to know how this particular site was used previously. If, for instance, we are considering this particular site for a gas station and three similar undertakings failed at this same site, we need to examine the proposed business in question more carefully. It would be inappropriate to think that the previous retailers could not make it but we can. If the site is not adequate, success in retailing is impossible. In analyzing the site's history, it is also critical to determine what happened to other retail establishments in the immediate area so we may know what is likely to happen to us. Knowing the proximity to other stores that are complementary to our proposed retail establishment is a powerful factor for us; we must be clear what is near to the site and whether a steady relationship with the stores that are near to the site that is being considered is likely to be synergistic. International Rug Imports is a case in question. The store had a very good selection of Turkish and Persian rugs at very good prices. It was located at a high-traffic corner of a regional shopping center. However, its location was between a drug store and a supermarket. People who are likely to buy expensive imported rugs are not likely to do their grocery shopping or go to drug stores in the same trip. International Rug Imports went out of business in less than six months.

Accessibility

The site is evaluated only on the basis of its proximity to prospective customers that may prove to be a costly error. Even though a good site must have reasonable proximity to prospective customers, it may have occasional or often excessive traffic congestion. Therefore, during certain times of the day it may not be very accessible. If the vehicular traffic is being analyzed for the site in question, at least five issues need to be clarified:

1. Is the site capable of generating consumer traffic?
2. What are the specific features that would enhance the attractiveness of our retail facility?
3. How safe is the area for pedestrians?
4. What is the expected growth potential of the pedestrian traffic?
5. What is the growth potential in the immediate trading area?

These are general questions. Each would lead to numerous additional questions that are specific and important for our retail venture. However, most of these are types of retailing specifics that need to be examined carefully as an area being evaluated.

Legal Aspects

Every potential and actual site has certain legal dimensions that need to be examined. These are, among others, zoning laws, landlord responsibilities, renter responsiveness, rent values, and land ownership.

How changeable the zoning laws are is the first critical question. If they are very changeable and we cannot plan how to cope with future competition, future zones, and future growth, we may have to stay away from a particular site. Similarly, zoning laws may change in such a way that they may enhance or hinder economic development. This could be rather dangerous.

Since most retailers are more likely to lease than build, responsibilities of the landlords in regard to maintaining the area, the facilities, and the specific building, that is being considered, are critical. If the landlords are not committed to upkeep—maintaining and improving buildings and grounds—then the retailer needs to stay away. Furthermore, if the management or the property owners are unrealistic in their demands about rent, maintenance, and other related areas, these matters could be very damaging to the prospective retailer.

Renter responsibilities need to be arrived at jointly rather than dictated by the landlord groups. Of course, the other renters' behavior can be critical for a prospective retailer. If, for instance, it is detected that other renters are not fulfilling their responsibilities of maintaining the physical facilities and surroundings and are considering leaving the premises, the proposed retail facility should be very hesitant to locate there.

Rent values can be and/or can become very unrealistic. In many cases when the properties are owned by absentee owners or property owners are leaving the area, they may charge exorbitant rental rates. Similarly, some property owners may tie the rents to the national price index, which may be too high for the particular community in question. The prospective retailer, in addition to being sensitive to these issues, must also be able to judge a reasonable rental rate by evaluating the strengths and weaknesses of a proposed site.

Finally, land and property ownership can create a major legal problem. For instance, if the owner dies and multiple heirs cannot agree on certain terms, the prospective retailer may find the situation very difficult.

ASSESSING MARKET POTENTIAL

Once the site is singled out, it is critical to assess what that site could generate in terms of sales volume. Earlier in this chapter we explored how much sales volume may be generated in the area under study, but all things being the same, the share of that volume for the proposed retail facility is the key question. Regarding the retail facility being planned, at least two approaches become critical: first, establishing an average size for the establishment, and second, measuring store saturation level which questions if the area has too much of one type of retailing. Average establishment size would depend upon dollar sales per square foot for each trade line, estimated total trade, and number of establishments in the area. The following formula could help conceptualize this issue:

$$\text{Average establishment size} = \frac{\text{Estimated total sales}}{\text{Dollar sales per sq. foot} \times \text{Number of stores}}$$

An exercise quantifying this formula is as follows: Assuming estimates indicate that convenience store sales in the area is $2,000,000. Sales per square foot in this type of retailing is $20.00. And in the area there are 50 stores that are similar to the proposed facility. Placing the numbers in the formula—2,000,000/(20 × 50) = 2,000—the rough estimated size of the proposed facility is around 2,000 square feet. Given the average size for the proposed retail facility, if we plan more than, say, doubling that we face a serious risk of not being able to sell enough.

Along with the average establishment, size, and store, saturation level in the area is also critical. The store saturation level indicates whether there are more than the necessary number of stores in the area and what the trend may be in this direction. Here it is considered the number of prospective customers and how much they spend on the line of merchandise in question and the number of stores dealing with that product line. The following formula can be used for store saturation evaluation:

$$\text{Store saturation level} = \frac{\text{Number of customers} \times \text{Average expenditures}}{\text{Number of retail establishments}}$$

Assuming, there are 10,000 prospective customers for our proposed supermarket and the average income is $25,000. National averages show that 30 percent of income is spent on food. Although these figures are hypothetical, the real figures would depend on where the proposed retail facility is planning on locating. Based on the above figures the formula would indicate that $10,000 \times 25,000 \times 30\% = 75,000,000$. If there are ten supermarkets in the area, the store saturation level would indicate that the expected total sales figure would be around $7,500,000 which is not enough for a supermarket. The area is already over-saturated. So the proposed store may not be satisfactory in terms of the prospective sales volume.

One additional and more specific method of evaluation of the site calls for establishing the total sales in the area in question as presented in Exhibits 6.2 and 6.3. Then approximating the square footage in the area of other similar stores is simply walking through the establishments. Knowing what the national averages are for the type of store in terms of sales per square foot, we can establish if the proposed site has the potential to yield a satisfactory sales volume, the average of which again is available nationally. This approach is discussed briefly in the following section.

Estimating Sales Potential for the Proposed Store

Once the area potential is established, then it becomes necessary to determine how much of this total can be the proposed store's sales volume. Here additional information relating to (1) demographics and income levels and (2) purchasing behavior and spending patterns of the people in the area needs to be examined.

Exhibit 6.7 illustrates an estimate of sales potential for the proposed store. Let us assume that the proposed retail establishment is an apparel store and, consecutively, about 10 percent of annual income

Exhibit 6.7   Sales Potential for the Proposed Store

Number of households in the retail trading area	1,500 households
	$\times$
Average annual income of the households in the trading area	$50,000
	$\times$
Amount of the income goes into purchasing the products sold by the store	10.0%
	$\times$
The estimated proportion of income spent on the product line that may be spent in the proposed store	30.0%
	$\times$
The proportion of this total will go to competing stores	(–) 10.0%
Sales potential of the proposed store (approximates rounded)	$2,400.00 per year

goes to apparel. Of that 10 percent, the proposed store is likely to capture about 30 percent, since there are only two other stores in the area. But a safety measure of an additional 10 percent is allocated for these stores. If the estimates are reasonable and the retail establishment performs well, the annual gross sales are expected to be around $2,400,000; this may be quite acceptable.

CAPITAL NEEDS ESTIMATION

Once we estimated that the proposed store could make around $2,400,000, it is critical to determine the capital needs of this project to get started. Our discussion so far has been only a means to an end. Without establishing the store's capital needs, there could not be a true assessment of this store's feasibility. In other words, the end cannot be assessed without estimating the expected profit margin after taxes.

When small businesses fail, the excuse given is often that the enterprise was undercapitalized. Unless there are adequate funds, a business should not get started. However, it is also possible that the business was not managed properly and, as a result, ran out of capital. Exhibit 6.8 provides some basic ballpark figures that can be used to establish the capital needs. First, let us assume that 60 percent of sales are the cost of goods sold. It is reasonable to assume a revolving credit of six months. Hypothetically, we assume that the inventory turnover rate, which indicates how many times the average inventory is sold in the course of a year, is about 3. Based on these inputs and the data in Exhibit 6.7 the following calculations take place. Sixty percent of $2,400,000 is $1,440,000. This number, divided by 3, would yield approximately $480,000. Since this is six months revolving credit, and inventory turnover rate is 3, $480,000 is divided by 6. This would yield $80,000 per month. This is what would be needed for two months of inventory.

It is also critical to realize that for about two months of operations the store is not likely to yield any profit. These two months must be covered. Forty percent of $2,400,000 is about $960,000, which is $80,000 per month, plus the two months equivalent is $160,000. This amount is two month's cost of operations. Although in Exhibit 6.8 the cost of operations is shown to be 23.8 percent, 40 percent was taken as a precautionary measure at the beginning. This brings the capital requirements to $160,000 + $160,000 which is equal to $320,000. In addition to operation costs for two months, there are preopening expenditures. These expenditures are not excessive since

Exhibit 6.8   Operating Expenditures in Percentages*

Net sales	100.0
Cost of goods sold	60.0
Cost of operations	23.8
Rent	2.9
Interest	0.7
Depreciation	0.8
Pensions	0.3
Other Promotion	14.4
Compensation	3.0
Taxes	1.3
Projected profit margin after taxes	3.3

*These types of figures are available at US Department of Commerce, Office of Small Business Administration.

the land and buildings are included in the rent. The site is likely to be made operational for the retailer by the landlord. However, there are some expenditure such as store layout, display windows, signs, promotional items, and others. Anywhere between 10 and 25 percent of the monthly revenues may be allocated for about two months. The monthly revenue is estimated to average around $200,000 ($2,400,000 divided by 12 = $200,000). Ten percent of $200,000 (two months revenue) is $40,000, which will be added to total capital requirements. Added on to $320,000, the total capital requirements will reach $360,000. It must be reiterated that preopening promotional activity is one of the most serious expense items. It is covered in the cost of operations.

Taking an industry average of profits for small and medium-sized stores, 3.3 percent after taxes and other expenditures yields about $79,000. If the capital requirements are about $360,000 and net profits $79,000, then about an average percent return would be $2,400,000 / $360,000 that will yield a 15 percent return on the investment. All things being equal, this may be a reasonable return for investment and the project in question can be looked upon favorably.

SUMMARY

Without proper location decisions a retailer cannot survive. It is, therefore, critical that major research activity goes into this phase of analysis. Seven steps are discussed in conjunction with this analysis: (1) identify the particular area, (2) delimit the trading area, (3) single out the site, (4) assess market potentials, (5) estimate sales potential, (6) estimate capital needs, and (7) decide whether to go ahead with the project or not.

Within these seven steps there are many activities. First, there is much that can be done in this all important analysis; therefore, additional creativity and effort will go a long way. Second, without careful analysis of capital needs and a reasonable approximation of return on investment, a store is taking a big risk. It is not necessarily true that the procedures presented in this chapter indicate a failsafe guaranteed approach, but they reduce the failure risk. Therefore, they must be considered very carefully.

7

Consumer Behavior and Retail Strategy

The small and medium-sized independent retailers' success is directly related to understanding consumer behavior, particularly the behavior of the store's customers and responding effectively. Here, the point must be made emphatically that understanding consumer behavior is not for the purpose of exploiting consumers, but to satisfy their needs better than retail giants who treat customers as simply numbers. The independent retailer's strength is to make sure that the customers, individually, are satisfied so that they will come back to the store again and again. The key to success is the creation of consumer value.

Understanding Consumer Behavior

Every retailer must understand what makes consumers behave the way they do. Although a retailer cannot change the internal workings of such behavior, a retailer can influence it by advertising and other attempts to communicate as well as making the shopping experience more pleasurable. Marketing strategies of the retailer must be in that direction. Although there is no single retail consumer behavior model, the model presented here is very functional and facilitates retail marketing strategies accordingly.

Exhibit 7.1 presents such a model. Consumer behavior, in conjunction with retailing, has three major phases: pre-purchase behavior, purchase behavior, and post-purchase behavior. The first explores just how consumers (preferably our customers) decide that they need certain products or services, or when they would like to go shopping. The second phase delves into how consumers (again preferably our customers) choose the stores, products, and brands as they are engaged in shopping. The third phase examines the thought process that will keep our customers happy or unhappy. The idea of course is to make sure that they are satisfied and they will be back to our place

Exhibit 7.1   Consumer Behavior as It Applies to Retailing

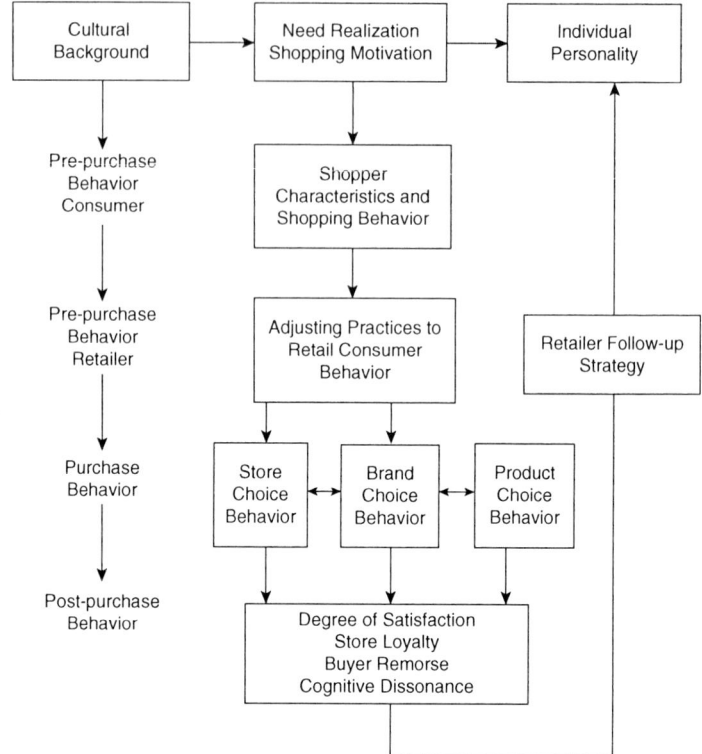

Source: Adapted and revised from Samli (2004).

of business. Dissatisfied customers develop cognitive dissonance (or buyer remorse). Post-purchase exploration and, if needed, corrective action would remedy the situation. But it must be reiterated that the causes of buyer remorse is understood and dealt with.

Consumer behavior as a discipline has made significant progress during the past four decades or so. Many models, explaining some of the most intimate aspects of this behavior, have surfaced, discussed, tested, and partially or fully incorporated into our general marketing knowledge base. Unfortunately, however, only a very small proportion of this research effort and knowledge base has been allocated to retailing. Thus, retailing still suffers from not receiving its fair share from our ever-increasing knowledge of consumer behavior (Samli 2004).

It is, therefore, clear that any attempt to understand and explain this very complex and dynamic retail consumer behavior, which is multiphase and influenced by multiple economic, political, and social factors, is invaluable. In the final analysis, it would enhance the contribution to the existing quality of life that retailing makes in the society. It must be reiterated that better utilization of consumer behavior knowledge would not only would enhance the contributions the retailing sector is making to the society, but also improve the success rate of retail establishments in terms of survival and profitability.

A critical point must be made regarding Exhibit 7.1. The pre-purchase behavior needs to be explored from the consumer point of view as well as the retailer point of view. If the retailer understands shopper characteristics and shopping behavior, he or she can identify retail consumer behavior patterns accordingly. This point is particularly important for small and medium-sized independent retailers for survival.

CULTURE, PERSONALITY, AND SHOPPING BEHAVIOR

The consumer behavior model presented in Exhibit 7.1 begins on one end with cultural background and ends with individual personality. Culture, according to many thinkers and researchers, is the basic force behind consumer behavior. It has been maintained that an individual is influenced by a culture screen which develops the personality and behavior pattern. Those two characteristics somewhat formulate consumption patterns and shopping behaviors. Stated differently, all people are products of a culture which is the link connecting people in a group or nation. As such, these people share similar values and broadly behave the same way. Thus, culture dictates behavior.

Based on these assertions, cultural background and personality must be considered simultaneously, and behavioral patterns must be analyzed accordingly. In the United States, there are many minorities such as Asian-Americans, Hispanic-Americans, and African-Americans. Additionally, there are subcultures among the majority, mainly based on economic and educational diversities. Though there have been many attempts to classify cultures or subcultures in conjunction with retailing, most cultural dichotomies and their impact on retail purchase behavior have not been as readily recognizable or applicable. Generalizations of all Americans liking lower prices and therefore they frequent discounting retailers is not exactly correct. Clearly, particularly small and medium-sized independents must be aware of cultural characteristics such as brand loyalty, appreciating ease of shopping, or detailed personal interaction among many others. These features are not generalized for a whole country.

Here, we dichotomize consumer behavior between individualistic and collectivistic subcultures (Samli 2012). Exhibit 7.2 examines these two dichotomous cultures as they relate to retailing. Consumers in an individualistic culture are more self-reliant. They are primarily affected by cognitive influences (facts, direct learning, and information received). Although at the periphery, they are also influenced by social class and hierarchy of needs, as indicated by Maslow (1964). That influence, the realization of perceived needs at the core of the purchasing process, is initiated by the individual. This is why self-service has been rather critical in major shopping complexes as well as in discount giants throughout the United States. Affective influences here, as opposed to cognitive influences which are beliefs and traditional values, play a less critical role.

The distinction between information and knowledge gathered by the individual versus emotional and traditional values instilled onto the individual would make a clear and important distinction as to how the retailer must behave in each. Studies have shown, for example, that while white American professional women rely on their own judgment, African-American counterparts rely more heavily on suggestions of store personnel. The same behavior pattern resembling the latter is observed in the behavior of Asian-Americans. Particularly, the first generation of this group shop in ethnic retail stores and are very close to store personnel, whereas the second generation show relatively less

Exhibit 7.2   Cultural Differences and Retail Shopping

Individualistic Consumer	Collectivistic Consumer
• Influenced primarily by cognitive forces. Makes up his/her mind based on the information collected	• Influenced by the group and its values. Affective influences and group reassures are more prominent
• Has the initiative to search for goods and services until they are found	• Economic necessities and preferences articulated by the group are critical
• Influenced more by hierarchy of needs and social class that the group to which he/she belongs	• Certain opinion leaders or family elders decide what is to be purchased when, where now and other details
• Sensitive to information regarding the store, product, and brand	• Sensitive to opinions and values of the group or opinion leaders regarding store product and brand
• Not typically loyal to store brand or product	• More store brand and product loyal
• In store uses own initiative and search process	• In store often follows store keepers directions

Source: Adapted and revised from Samli (2004).

ethnicity. As was mentioned earlier in this book, since minority populations are growing more proportionately, such observations followed by certain practices will enhance the success probabilities of small-scale retailers by emphasizing ethnicity and personalized service.

On the other hand, other individuals such as extended family elders or other opinion leaders influence consumers in collectivistic subcultures. They more often learn from others based on affective influences. Economic necessities play a critical role in their behavior patterns and values. Certain beliefs and values (affective influences) are instilled in individuals by others in their immediate circles (Samli 2012). These influences have very significant retailing implications. Most minorities in the United States display many aspects of this type of consumer behavior with some minor variations perhaps because they are more cohesive and interdependent.

In these two different cultures, consumer behavior regarding retailing is significantly different; therefore, retailers must develop certain practices to cater to these differing behaviors and resultant needs.

The two separate cultures as indicated in Exhibit 7.2 display differences in their retail shopping behavior and these differences must be utilized carefully by retailers. Their retail practices must be adjusted to these differences in buying behavior. The six key points dealing with the differences depicted in Exhibit 7.2 should lead to the following retail practices.

First, in addressing individualistic consumer behavior, there will be more emphasis on advertising directly to the individual consumer. It is quite likely that more e-tail advertising will be used in this respect as well. Here, since the individual behaves by cognitive influences more information may be imparted so that individuals could decide what to buy and where. The collectivistic consumer, on the other hand, will be reached through advertising to the opinion leaders and family elders.

Second, the individualistic consumer will exercise more initiative to search for products and stores than the collectivistic consumer. The latter will be influenced, again, by others. They will choose stores that are recommended to them by opinion leaders and family elders.

Third, individualistic consumers also have values and the hierarchy of needs. But, in general, they rely on information they gather on their own. Collectivistic consumers get their values more readily from the groups that they are involved in.

Fourth, if individualistic consumers are making decisions according to their need perception, then they are likely to be more sensitive to information about products, stores, and brands. The collectivistic consumers, on the other hand, are making decisions either for others, primarily opinion leaders and/or family elders who would also need information, or under the influence of the group. They may not need as much of the type of information they will follow that coincides with the group's desires.

Fifth, store loyalty of individualistic consumers can easily be questioned since they may go by newly received information which may indicate that the other store may have something better. Collectivistic consumers are more likely to be loyal to store brand and product.

Finally, individualistic consumers are activity oriented. They prefer to explore on their own in a self-service setting. They prefer to do their own analysis and comparisons. They gather their own information. Collectivistic consumers are attribute oriented. They prefer to talk to store keepers, sales people, and others about the store, product, and brand features, especially in department stores and boutiques. They go more by impressions given to them by opinion leaders, family elders, or store keepers than the information they could gather.

As can be seen, these features and pronounced differences can easily guide retailers in their retailing marketing activities. Particularly small- or medium-scale independent retailers must know their cliental and must cater to their needs.

CONTRAST IN IN-STORE BEHAVIOR

As mentioned earlier, two somewhat opposing in-store behaviors are identified here. These are attribute orientated and activity orientated. They lead to noticeable contrasts between in-store behaviors of two culturally different consumer groups. Exhibit 7.3 displays some of the key contrasts between the two.

Attribute orientation, which is tied to collectivistic consumer behavior, pays attention to the detail about store features in terms of store layout and features along with the salespeople who are reinforcing these features. Collectivistic consumers ask store attendants and salespeople for advice and direction. The individualistic consumer on the other hand adapts activity orientation that focuses on the individual's own efforts to shop around and find things in the store. They focus more on self-service along with more self-effort to accumulate information about the store, merchandise, and brands. This behavior is different from the attribute orientation. The retailer must know which group he or she is mostly dealing with, and the retail facility and its personnel should be somewhat ready for both groups. Discount giants do not care about such behavior differences. They offer a large

Exhibit 7.3   In-Store Shopper Behavior

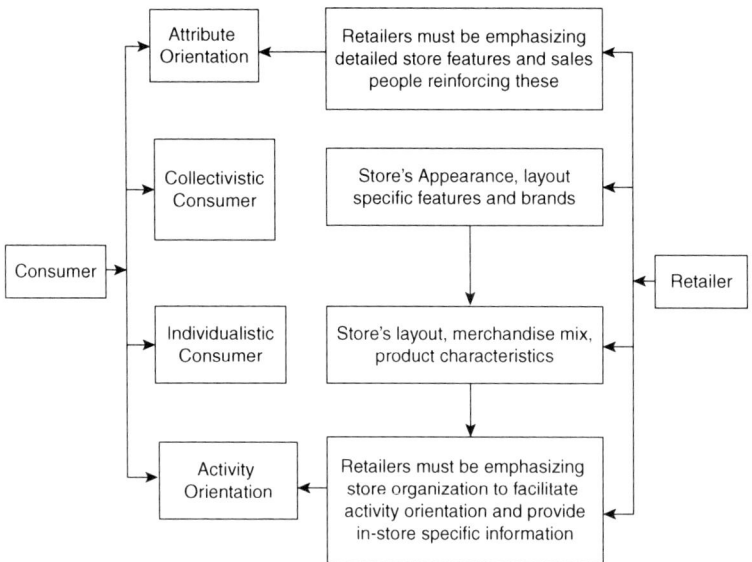

variety of products at discount prices and treat their customers as mass numbers. Small and medium-sized independents must make a major effort in dealing with both consumer groups and personalizing, meaning paying special attention to each customer. The retailer must have a good idea about the target market and how the members in that group are likely to shop. This means the store's appearance and features along with the personnel are to be considered carefully and be prepared for both attribute and activity orientation. Similarly, in-store logistics, which deals with the merchandise mix, asks how and where it is displayed in the store, needs to accommodate these two separate consumer orientations. Finally, the information flows in and out of the store, along with promotional effort of the retail establishment needing to be adjusted depending on whether the primary concern is collectivistic consumer behavior or individualistic consumer behavior. Social media communication also must consider these two consumer behaviors to promote the store efficacy.

Even though these two cultural camps have different reasons and approaches to patronizing retail stores and shopping, in general terms they still have certain basic shopping motives. Although some of these motives are somewhat similar, they surface in different forms for the two cultural groups or subgroups.

CONSUMER'S SHOPPING MOTIVES AND RETAILER'S RESPONSE

Every retailer should realize that not all consumers patronize a retail facility for the same reasons. In fact, people frequent retail facilities for different reasons. Retailers must realize just why people shop and more importantly, why they shop in the retail facility where they shop.

Need, realization, and shopping motivation are presented in Exhibit 7.1 as the first consideration. Just how people realize that they do need certain products or services and what it would take for consumers to be motivated to go to certain retail establishments to shop are extremely critical issues.

A few attempts have been made to determine the shopping motives that consumers experience (Samli 2004). Ten different motives have been identified as the most important factors behind retail shopping. These are:

1. Diversion—consumers need to get away to break up their dull and uninspiring daily routines.
2. Self-gratification—a special stimulation of the individual's psyche is created by the shopping process within a certain ambiance (Hulter, Broweus, and Van Dijk (2009).
3. Learning about new trends or fashions—since there are new products and services that are entering the retail sector along with new fashions, individuals can learn more about them as they shop around.
4. Physical activity—walking around in large shopping complexes may be the only exercise and relaxation some people may receive in their hectic lives.
5. Sensory stimulation—by seeing, touching, smelling, or trying on the products, individuals can experience sensory satisfaction.
6. Social experiences outside the home—socializing with friends and other customers, going to shop with friends, and interacting with store personnel all provide special motivation.
7. Pleasure of negotiation and choice selection—being able to compare, contrast, and negotiate the terms of the purchase in order to find best buys is a critical stimulator.
8. Satisfying clearly identified needs and wants—effort made to satisfy needs by shopping is a critical foundation of retailing.
9. Peer pressures or opinion leader influence—individuals are influenced by others to buy certain things to be part of new trends.
10. To satisfy shopping needs efficiently—being able to shop efficiently for most pressing needs is an important motivator.

As is specified in Exhibit 7.1 earlier, pre-purchase behavior begins with need realization which is to be satisfied with shopping motivation. The ten shopping motives discussed here are also presented in Exhibit 7.4. In the exhibit, the retail practices that are appropriate for each shopping motive are further specified. Implementing retail strategies with such practical activities give a great advantage to the individual retailer. However, the retail practices section of Exhibit 7.4 must be carefully understood and implemented. These practices differentiate the stores and create differential congruence for a retail establishment. Each retail establishment must consider which one of the ten shopping motives is most appropriate for its particular clientele and then must decide how its retail practices must be implemented in order to cater to its customers to satisfy shopping motives. Certainly, in many cases the retail customers could have not one but a combination of these purchases motives.

Exhibit 7.4   Shopping Motives versus Retail Practices

Shopping Motives	Retail Practices
1. Diversion from daily routine	Making the store visit exciting
2. Self-gratification	Helping customers to make good purchase decisions by offering choices and giving good information
3. Learning about new trends or fashions	Carrying most up-to-date products properly displayed along with providing good information.
4. Physical activity	Customers can walk around freely and safely as they look or try out products
5. Sensory stimulation	Attractive arrangements and appearances to feel, try on, or try out products
6. Social experiences outside the home	Having an opportunity to socialize in the store with the personnel and other customers. Having special sales events
7. Pleasure of negotiation and choice selection	Giving an opportunity to negotiate, analyze, compare products and discuss them with others
8. Satisfying clearly identified needs and wants	Making sure that the store is known to carry certain products all the time, helping customers to shop quickly
9. Peer pressures or opinion leader influences	The store carries certain products that are subject to influences from others new models, new fashions, etc.
10. To satisfy shopping needs effectively	Proper pre-purchase communication, adequate emphasis on e-trade, in store adjustments such as express lanes, etc.

In a general sense, any one of the ten motives presented here may not play a more critical role in the consumer's shopping behavior than any other in the retailer's target groups. The retailer must know that. This situation may be completely reversed in that some of these motives, in the specific market segments the retailer is dealing with, may be extremely important. Of course, the retail must know that to survive and prosper. Finally, it must be understood that these ten motives are not totally mutually exclusive, in that they may interact with or complement one another. Having analyzed these ten shopping motives leads to the conclusion that the survival and success of the retail establishment is vitally connected to them. The retailer must understand and cater to shopper characteristics that are triggered by these ten shopping motives. Without understanding and adjusting the retail practices it would be difficult, if not impossible, to succeed. The retail must not only satisfy the customers' needs but must delight them. That is the essence of differential congruence.

GROUPING SHOPPERS

In addition to shopping motives of their own, individuals have major differences in their shopping practices. Exhibit 7.5 illustrates an attempt to group shoppers and connect them to the shopping motives which are presented in Exhibit 7.4. Although the classification of the groups and their shopping motives is somewhat arbitrary, it is maintained here that any retailer that can look at the store's clientele and group them, connect them to certain shopping motives, and identify their retail behaviors which can be effectively used for these groups is bound to be successful. It takes objective analysis and understanding as well as caring for customers to be successful in retailing. Each retailer may find variations, additions, and deletions in the classification presented in Exhibit 7.5. The classification presented in Exhibit 7.5 is composed of many earlier attempts. However, the present author considers it very functional and realistic. Although the sum total percentages add up to 100 percent, a typical retailer may be working with only one or two of these seven categories of people. A special comment about e-trade is in order here. There has been a significant increase in this particular activity. It is likely to increase further in the near future. In Exhibit 7.5 this is identified as the activity of safe shoppers. This activity is connected to increased home delivery. However, just who buys through the Internet and why this group needs to be identified separately are critical questions. The present author believes that this group needs home delivery much of the time. The independent

Exhibit 7.5 Shopper Groupings

Shopper	Description	Purchase Motivation
Agreeable Shoppers 23%	Lower-middle income, shopping at discount stores, much mass media exposure. Brand loyal for everything	Clearly identified needs and wants, specific pressures
Practical Shoppers 22%	Research purchases in advance, looking for best deals, middle income, younger, better educated, women. Buy modern frills. Not too brand loyal	Pleasure of bargaining, learning about new trends. Extensive Internet search
Trendy Shoppers 17%	Impulse buyers. Prefer latest fads. Frequent fashion boutiques. Mostly young. Not much brand loyalty. Need many products. Prefer imports	Self-gratification, sensory stimulation
Value Shoppers 15%	Cost conscious. Brand loyal. Prefer old, accepted products and brands. Frequent department stores. Older, higher than average income. Consider shopping a chore	Clearly identified needs. Satisfying shopping needs efficiently
Top-of-the-line Shoppers 10%	Shop at upscale department stores. Equate quality with reputation. Older, highest median income. Prefer imports	Social experiences, diversion, self-gratification
Safe Shoppers 9%	Prefer familiarity. Tradition. Do not like shopping. Go to well-known mass merchandisers. Use e-trade	Clearly identified needs. Specific pressures to shop. Home delivery
Status Shoppers 5%	Impractical. Like new gadgets. Second highest median income. Spend much time on shopping, but also buy on impulse	Physical activity, social experiences, self-gratification, learning about new trends, satisfying shopping needs efficiently

Source: Adapted and revised from Samli (2004).

small-scale retailers can be using this activity as a special advantage since the retail giants, particularly discounters, do not get involved in that activity. Safe shoppers, among other features, do not like the physical activity attached to shopping. This does not mean that cyberspace cannot be used for contacting and informing other groups. It simply means that this group, that is, safe shoppers, is more active in e-trading than other groups.

It is strongly suggested that proactive independent retailers generate their own information not only grouping their customers and identifying their purchase motives, but also communicating individual customers and communicating with them, if possible, individually through cyberspace. Here, stores may promote themselves, available product alternatives, brands that are available, and other services. Personalizing individual customers is a critical advantage that smaller independents can use. The proactive independents must be always on the lookout for additional information that will enable them to satisfy their customers and encourage them to come back.

Needless to say, pre-purchase activities, post-purchase activities, and behavior patterns (Exhibit 7.1) are extremely critical, particularly smaller-scale independents, for survival. Although three major phases of shopper behavior may differ from one retail complex to another, understanding these and manipulating them is the key differential congruence builder leading to retail success.

THE PURCHASE PROCESS

Need realization on the part of the prospective customer begins with perception. The typical consumer is constantly exposed to mass media and other types of information and promotion. Here, once again, the proactive independent retailer must find a way to identify the retailing complex and attract attention of prospective customers.

Each individual is different; therefore, the messages and information received are interpreted somewhat differently. As the individual decodes these messages and information, a purchase need recognition surfaces. This need recognition is further interpreted by the individual in terms of a product or service, a brand, and a store. This interpretation by the individual indicates a powerful job by retail marketing. The enhancement of the purchase need can take place at both the conscious and subconscious levels. When a consumer receives a stimulus that is related to shopping, it is received at a threshold from which it may penetrate the conscious or subconscious levels. At the subconscious level, the stimulus may establish an image of the product, brand, or store. At the conscious level, however, it may enhance the image of the product, brand, or store, or all three. The subconscious appeal, if intentionally attempted, as in the case of subliminal advertising, is not legal and is likely to create legal or ethical problems in the long run. Thus, the retailer will do better by attempting to penetrate the conscious level with faster and more tangible results. However, it may be maintained that any message or stimulus would have, at least nominally, a subconscious appeal as well. That appeal, if proper and not likely to create a future controversy, could accumulate and make the retailer's short-run efforts much more effective by creating a synergistic impact with the efforts to penetrate conscious perception of customers. The x, y, z store is cheaper and exercises conscious perception of its customer needs; it also has the most knowledgeable sales people and gives subconscious message.

A consumer's buying behavior starts with a stimulus perception. As this perception brings about problem recognition, the consumer begins acquiring some information or receiving certain messages that are related to the recognized problem. Since consumer information is critical for the retailer, the retailer must understand the consumer's information search process.

Information regarding retail shopping comes from different sources. Those who have lived in an area longer may get more information from friends and relatives than those who are new in the area. Note: my earlier book was published in 2004 when we had not heard anything about social media which carries messages among consumers. This is a new challenge and a valuable tool for the limited scale independent retailers. Most retail giants at this point of writing this book do not pay much attention to social media. But consumers receive more and better information from other consumers through social media than the traditional mass media.

One might question if the traditional "Weber's law" would work with social media conditions. Weber's law states that as the stimulus intensities get stronger, it will take more of a change in a new stimulus to be noticed. In other words, for a stimulus to become more important, it must have a "just noticeable difference" that must be somewhat more of an attention getter than other stimuli (Wilkie 1994). Every retailer must explore attention-getting activities, including social media influences that will make a difference.

As the problem, or the need recognized by the prospective customer, is a desire for a service or a product, this recognition may have degrees of intensity. The more successful the retail marketing strategy is, the greater is the recognized problem's intensity. If the retailer is capable of solving important consumer problems, it implies that there is a successful retailing strategy at work. Obviously the problem needs to be intense enough so that the consumer feels the need to buy the product or service in question. The greater the intensity of the recognized problem, the greater are the possibilities for the brand image and store image to become critical reinforces of that intensity and therefore influence the consumer to frequent the store. Of course, some or all of the shopping motives, discussed earlier, also come into play, meaning that the retailer must keep all of the shopping motives in mind all the time.

As the stimuli are perceived and the problem is recognized, consumers begin an information search. All prospective customers search for some information. This search could be conscious or unconscious. A systematic search for information is conscious whereas information coming in haphazardly would be unconscious. But since consumer shopping behavior is learned, shoppers must have a basic learning process that is stimulated by a conscious consumer information search. Shopping for groceries at, say, Publix or buying home repair supplies at Home Depot or buying shoes at Payless Shoe Source all call for basic learning processes that lead in the direction of store loyalties. However, as discussed in Exhibit 7.2, the differences in cultural backgrounds lead individualistic consumers to search and receive information differently from collectivistic consumers.

Every consumer goes through a search process prior to shopping. This process is composed of two separate search motivations, internally triggered and externally triggered. The search motivation leads to a two-step search activity, out-of-store and in-store. If the search activity is internally triggered, individualistic consumer may lean in the direction of store-disseminated information. This may further be connected to cognitive influences by mass media or social media. This may lead to an external search for a suitable outlet for the product or service to be purchased.

On the other hand, collectivistic consumers are motivated by external affective influences which are further reinforced by store employees or sales people's influences. These lead to further internal searches for goods within the retail complex. The clear distinction between the individualistic versus collectivistic consumers is that the first group relies on self-perception for both external and internal searches, whereas the second group is influenced by others for both external and internal searches.

This information search is very closely related to store, product, and brand selections. Here the retailer must make sure that more being promised than delivered is a tremendous handicap. The store, product, brand, and service must be consistently good and congruent. The retailer that promises something but delivers something else is not likely to last long in the marketplace.

As indicated in Exhibit 7.1, the retail consumer shopping process does not end at the point where the purchase transaction is completed. Peters (1989) stated that it is five times more costly to get new customers than to keep current customers happy so that they repeat purchases. Festinger (1957) generated the theory of "cognitive dissonance" which is as relevant today as it was then. This theory relates to what is called, in common parlance, "buyer's remorse." If, for whatever reason, a customer develops second thoughts about a recent purchase and does not feel very good about shopping in a specific store and/or about the merchandise that was purchased, then there is cognitive dissonance, and the consumer is not likely to come back.

If the retailer cannot eliminate such post-purchase blues, then that particular establishment is in deep trouble. The problem may be generated by extreme pressure-selling tactics, less than adequate customer services, questionable quality merchandise, but perhaps above all, by a lack of follow-up. To counter cognitive dissonance, the retailer must find out just what caused the problem and eliminate it immediately. But, regardless of occurring episodes of cognitive dissonance, it is a very good policy to have an automatic follow-up to keep the customer satisfied.

The retail store must conduct post-purchase exploration, in store or out of store, with cards, phone calls, mail surveys, and e-mails to find out how satisfied their customers are, if they are planning to come back, and if they would recommend the store to others. Similarly, stores must be sensitive to customer complaints. It is possible to determine if there is customer attrition based on post-purchase dissatisfaction. The retailer must be able to determine the extent of post-purchase attrition and stop it quickly. Contacting the customer after purchase, exercising liberal return policies, and reemphasizing customer recourse practices of the store are all counter-buyer's remorse practices.

IMPLICATIONS FOR SEGMENTATION

Nobody more than a retailer in the market system can appreciate the fact that markets are not homogeneous. They are composed of segments which are: identifiable, measurable, significant, accessible, actionable, and sustainable. Almost any basic marketing text book would have some version of these features discussed.

A retailer, as seen in this chapter, deals with submarkets, which are market segments that are identified as shopper groups, and each one of these shopper groups is influenced by one or more purchase motives that have been discussed.

However, an attempt to identify the target markets that a retailer deals with as agreeable, practical, and the like is inadequate because this classification is not tangible enough. In addition to attitudes or behavior patterns, market segments need to be identified on the basis of demographics and other observable and tangible common characteristics. Exhibit 7.6 presents basic criteria for retail segmentation. Perhaps the most important message the exhibit relays is that not only are there many ways of identifying and interacting with market segments, it is almost impossible to cater to all. Even Walmart, the largest retailer in the world at the writing of this book, does not bring in or appeal to the market segment that frequents Neiman Marcus or Bergdorf Goodman. At the same time, it is rather dangerous for a retailer to focus on one market segment alone. Even a more specialized retailer, such as a chocolatier or a gift shop, is likely to appeal

Exhibit 7.6   Basic Criteria for Retail Segmentation

Criteria	Examples in Retail Practice
Ethnic or Cultural	
Ethnic groups	Spanish speaking shopping facilities
Certain subcultures	An overall Asian shopping complex
Demographics	
Income	High-income market vs. low-income market
Age	Elderly market, children's market
Education and occupation	Highly educated sophisticates
Sex	Male or female consumers
Sociological	
Social groups	Yuppies, WASPs, Generation X
Racial differences	African-Americans, Asian-Americans, Hispanics
Behavioral Measures	
Lifestyles	Jet-setters
Life cycles	Empty-nesters, young married couples
Attitudes	People who collect, people who like gadgetry
Store Loyalty	Those who buy certain products more often
Heavy users of certain products	
Regulars	
Loyals	
Benefit	Expected satisfaction by patronizing that store
Benefits sought	Satisfaction from the store or the product directly
Direct benefits received	Satisfaction delayed as in gifts or health foods
Greater vs. lesser benefits	Those who have improved health from a health spa
Geography	
Distances	Those who live nearby vs. those who travel a distance
Reputation of the location	Fashionable areas of town
In shopper vs. out shopper	The area's ability to attract from neighboring communities

Source: Adapted and revised from Samli (2004).

to multiple market segments. Therefore, it is reasonable that a retail store targets more than one segment. Sometimes these segments are rather small and readily identifiable. These small markets are niches. A retailer that is catering to a specific niche can be rather profitable. However, some niches may not last very long based on social trends and unexpected desires or preferences. It must be reiterated that markets are not homogeneous and it is critical that the retailer is treating these market segments differently depending upon each segment's needs and behaviors. Exhibit 7.6 illustrates how different segments may be treated. The retailer must be very alert to detect the market segment or segments that are being dealt with and act accordingly. It is extremely critical not only to understand the importance of segmentation, but also to develop makeable and effective practices to deal with these segments.

Retail Segmentation Process

Although most of the material presented in this chapter is applicable to retail segmentation, there is a logical sequence also implied which the retailer must follow. At the beginning of the chapter, a retail consumer behavior model is presented. Based on the premise of a detectable consumer behavior pattern, consumers are grouped. This attempt to group consumers identified the retailing tools that can be used for these groups. Next an analysis is presented to identify just what motivates the consumer to engage in retail shopping activity. These sequential steps become particularly actionable when segmentation criteria are introduced.

For instance, if Asian-American shoppers, motivated by clearly identified needs and specified pressures by others, are frequenting the store more than other identifiable groups, then the store may resort to ethnic or cultural segmentation. More people from this group will likely frequent the store if proper appeal is employed to attract this target market. Thus, from consumer behavior to segmentation, more analysis must take place. But the end result is greater consumer value, which translates into profits. In other words, differential congruence is achieved, and both parties are happy.

Summary

Retailing deals with consumer behavior; understanding this behavior is a must. Proactive retail strategies can easily work with consumer behaviors, leading to customer satisfaction and retailing profits.

Consumer behavior in retailing is first related to cultural background. In this chapter, collectivistic versus individualistic consumer behaviors are distinguished. These are culture driven and lead to different retail strategies. Over and beyond the cultural background retail purchase behaviors have pre-purchase and post-purchase phases. In each phase the retailer must be cognizant of the fact that much proactive retail strategic behavior is required of the retailer for customers to be happy enough to return and recommend the store to friends.

In responding to consumer behavior effectively, the retailer must understand that there are ten clearly identifiable shopping motives. Each motive is dealt with in certain specific retail practices.

This chapter also deals with a very important topic, segmentation. Analyzing consumer behavior leads in the direction of segmenting the market. Different criteria are used for retail segment identification. The retailer must be in a position to decide which of these criteria are most useful for their understanding of the segments that are being dealt with.

Finally, each retailer must understand that there are shopper groups, and each group may be influenced by certain purchase motives. Once these motives are understood, the retailer may decide how these motives must be treated so that current customers will be happy. This is five times less costly than trying to get new customers.

Appendix to Chapter 7

THE HIGH TOUCH EFFECT

Naisbitt (1982) published a book titled *Megatrends*. One of the megatrends was balancing high tech and high touch. Samli and Choi (2014) have conducted a study based on the increasing high-tech effect needing more and more high touch. This is based on the assumption that many people are spending so much time on their computers that they have an increasing need for other people (high touch).

Two matching consumer groups were interviewed. The first group evaluated the certain store characteristics of the local Walmart. The second group evaluated the same store characteristics of a local mid-size department store. Both groups were very familiar with both of the stores. Five store characteristics were explored: reliability of sales people, responsiveness of sales people, assurance given by the store, empathy displayed for consumer needs in each store, and finally the tangibles including appearance and layout of each store. Survey results indicated that the department store was preferred. Respondents indicated that they will frequent the department store knowing that prices are higher there. The study indicated that service and people may be preferred over discount prices at least sometimes. This is connected to Exhibit 7.4. Diversion from daily routine, the author believes that increasing high-tech exposure is creating a stronger need for high touch. This is one of the key points of this book. Small and medium independent retailers can gain an edge over discounters with personal and service components.

The study of discounter versus department store comparison indicated that services in department store sometimes are preferred to discounted prices. Thus, smaller independents must pay more attention to services they offer (Exhibit 7.A).

Exhibit 7.A   Consumer's Comparison of Discount versus Department Store

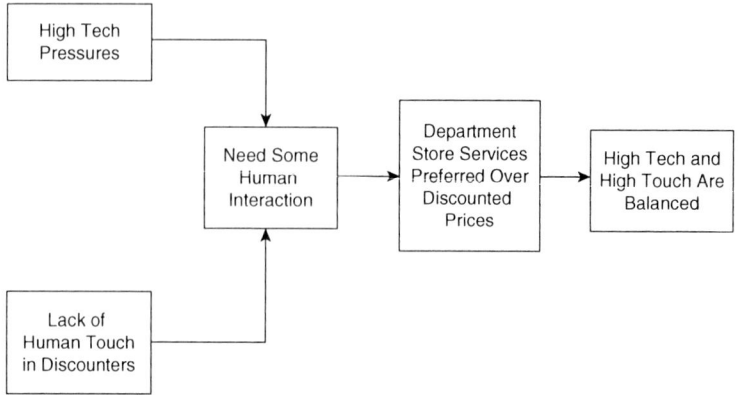

8

STRATEGY ALTERNATIVES

Having a game plan is the strategy which implies being proactive in fulfilling certain goals. Of course, these goals primarily revolve around being proactive and catering to the particular target market in the most favorable manner. This means providing goods and services in a most favorable terms. In doing so, the retailer can achieve competitive advantage and customer loyalty. Developing competitive advantage and gaining customer loyalty demonstrates that the retail establishment has developed differential congruence which means it is helping its customers to improve their lifestyles, and, of course, simultaneously improving its chances of survival and success.

THE THINKING OF THE RETAIL STRATEGIST

It must be clearly understood that, particularly in small-scale retailing, all owner-managers are strategists. They have to have a strategic plan to implement and reinforce their proactive orientation. The retail strategist will put together a game plan and implement it by using the retail mixes. This game plan, if successful, will make the store popular, catering to the target market effectively, while differentiating the store from its competitors, all in all creating a differential congruence. Unfortunately, many owner-managers are so busy with day-to-day activities; they do not make time to strategize. In such cases, the strategy is not planned and implemented; it just happens. This leaves the store not being proactive, but at best being reactive, and sadly, mostly being inactive. Strategic inactivity is a dangerous status for a retail establishment. Survival and related profitability, in such cases, become rather questionable.

Being a strategist is not just a process that happens automatically. All small retailers must think of a strategy and how to implement it, and as such they must go beyond their day-to-day manual activities so that they can think and plan.

Exhibit 8.1 Strategic Decision Process

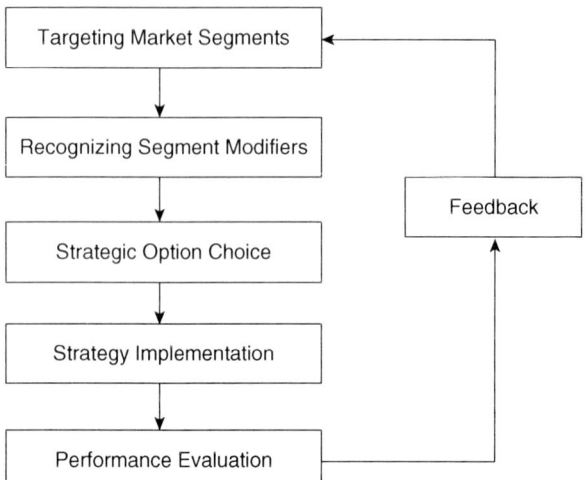

The strategic decision process goes through at least five stages as it is presented in Exhibit 8.1. Targeting market segments is the starting point that was discussed in chapter 7. At any given time the retailer must realize that there are external modifiers changing the existing targeted segments as time goes by. There are at least five such modifiers that are influencing market segments and discussing change. These changes would influence the retailing activity in that segment. The five segment modifiers are:

- Demographics: A continuous shift of population to the southeast, southwest, and west, for example, is changing the makeup of the retail markets. Additionally, changing age distribution and ethnic modifications are all important.
- New values: A growing concern about the environment, increasing interest in green products, consumer safety considerations, and recycling are playing critical roles.
- Economic realities: A noticeable decrease in the income of the middle class, outsourcing well-paying jobs, increasing consumer sophistication, and increasing the length of work week are creating changes in retailing.
- Escalating competition: Retail competition is changing as discounters and giants are taking over. Additionally, e-tailing, telemarketing, and nonstory retailing are increasing.

- New realities: As the middle class disappears, retail markets are becoming more fragmented. One-stop shopping and discount wholesaling are gaining more momentum. Older consumers and dual pay-check families are requiring more convenience also; other changes are taking place.

There are many other developments that are directly or indirectly influencing the retailing sector. These are all segment modifiers. The individual retailer must be very much aware of these for survival. The next step in Exhibit 8.1 is the identification and choice of a retail strategy.

TYPES OF STRATEGIES

Targeting segments and identifying the modifiers, if any, in action would help to decide what strategy, that is, the game plan, is most suitable for the retail establishment. Of course, these strategy options are always subject to change if needed. Six strategy options are identified here—general merchandising, segmenting, positioning, niching, category killing, and guerrilla fighting.

General Merchandiser

The retailer's strategy in this case is aggregating the market. This strategy can also be named mass retailing. Typically, general merchandisers start with merchandise mixes similar to those of competitors. The assumption here is that the market is large enough and that anybody can capture a portion of it by imitating others. For decades Sears, Montgomery Ward, and others thrived on convenience, variety, and one-stop shopping. These retailers made a wide assortment of products available at their relatively convenient locations where one-stop shopping and scrambled merchandising took place. On a much smaller scale, many country stores located at the edge of small towns in rural America still exercise this particular strategy. During the past two decades or more, discounters entered this category and over and beyond one-stop shopping and variety, they offered more much discounted prices. Thus, this general strategy uses goods (no service) mix, pricing mix, and logistics mix. Their advertising, if any, dwells upon these features and is rather informative. Segmentation is not extensively exercised by this group.

Differentiator

Although the differentiator may start with the premise that all consumers are basically alike, in reality they recognize that they may appeal to these consumers through different combinations of retail mixes. Here the strategy leads in the direction of generating a competitive edge by being different from competitors. In addition to differentiating the store with different retail mixes, retailers may add such features as credit, gift wrapping, delivery, extended store hours, liberal return policy, eating facilities, fashion shows, entertainment, and the like. Advertising and other promotional activity, including social media, must dwell upon these features. All in all, the strategy is geared to creating a store image that will distinguish the store from competitors. A differentiator, however, does not think of matching the store's unique features specifically with a specific target market's self-image and unique desires. A differentiator is still a generalist and does not create a tight differential congruence. The differentiator tells everybody "me different." While Walmart and Costco are general merchandisers and not very different in their market orientations, Home-Depot or Office-Depot are differentiators—they used much different merchandise mixes than Walmart or Costco.

Segmenter

If the retailer realizes that markets are not homogeneous, he or she starts thinking along the lines of trading areas that are composed of several homogeneous submarkets. Each of these is a segment where needs, purchase motives, and behavior patterns are quite uniform. The retailer targets one or more of these segments. Such a segmentation strategy in retailing has not been as rapid and as sophisticated as manufacturers' segmentation activity has been.

However, market segmentation is becoming more and more widespread among retailers. As more small retailers enter the arena, there will be a more noticeable exercise in segmenting, which will enhance consumer value generation in those identified segments. The Limited, Gap and Payless shoes are all examples of specialty retail chains that appeal to carefully defined market segments. Particularly at the higher economic level, some department stores are also trying to segment. Bloomingdales, Marshall Fields, and Macy's are obvious examples of department store chains that are involved in segmentation. Successful segmentation, by definition, generates differential congruence.

Positioner

A positioner strategist starts with orienting itself in the market place vis-à-vis specific competitors. Originally, Walmart positions itself somewhat below Sears, so that it could appeal to the fast-growing lower middle class as opposed to the somewhat shrinking upper middle class to which Sears appeals. Burger King positioned itself head to head with McDonald's. Wendy's positioned itself slightly above these two. One can detect such positioning strategy in almost all retailing situations. The critical point here is the deliberateness of this positioning activity. A retailer's positioning of itself without planning or even intending to do so is not quite as effective as a deliberate positioning strategy such as Target exercises. Target stores are and have been attempting to take some customers away from Sears and some from Walmart by positioning itself between the two. This has been very successful for Target.

Nicher

A nicher starts strategizing by identifying a carefully defined corner of the market. This corner of the market may barely have room for one retailer, meaning that there may not be much competition if the retailer entered this segment successfully. The nicher assumes that it can do the best job of satisfying the needs here and profiting from catering well to this carefully defined corner of the market. In this case, by doing a good job, the retailer preempts future competitors. The nicher is a very specific segmenter who is much closer to the markets, from general nutrition centers (GNC) catering to the health and body-building segments of the market, to a store in one small community or a retailer catering primarily the ethnic group of Hispanic immigrants are typical examples. Nichers must adjust the offerings very sharply to the needs of very well defined corners of the market.

This is rather a recent strategy that is still emerging. A category killer is a segmenting discounter. It starts with the orientation that, regardless of differences in their needs orientation, values, or buying behaviors, consumers truly go for bargains; in economic difficult times this orientation increases significantly. All people desire some product lines and many choices in each line. For instance, everyone buys a toy or two; therefore, Toys-R-Us, up to now, has been a very successful category killer. A category killer maintains better merchandise mixes with greater variety at lower prices and believes that whatever the competitors do, it can do better, which means, primarily, cheaper. Retail chains such as Home Depot and Books-A-Million may be considered to be category killers. Their successful activity, by definition, implies that they enjoy a very successful state of differential congruence. There are a number of areas where category killers are trying to establish their existence. Among these the brewery industry may be experiencing such a situation with a number of relatively new beers.

Guerrilla Fighter

Guerrilla fighting may be considered a strategic posture that is quite appropriate for small retailers and small manufacturers alike. Those who have limited budgets but great will to survive are willing to do whatever it takes to survive. They fight for existence and put in a great deal of effort to satisfy their customers. What they lack in resources, variety, and credit is compensated for by personal service, and relationship marketing. These establishments are managed hands-on, and change as conditions change. A small men's apparel shop, in time, may become a major center of uniforms, or a women's ready-to-wear clothing store may become an apparel store primarily catering to older women. Personal touches such as starting a fifty-plus club, sending birthday presents to members, or giving a percentage refund on all credit cards can be considered positive examples of guerrilla fighting strategies (Samli 2004).

Consider, for instance, the following: A caller in Florida is talking to a local florist on the phone. The caller says, "I would like to send two dozen roses to North Carolina. How much would that cost?" The store quotes a price. The caller replies, "Isn't this a bit too high?" The store spokesperson answers, "Maybe you should call someplace else." The caller gets two other estimates. Both are about half the price the first store quoted. The customer is lost to the store, probably for good. The customer will not call the first store again. With a small retail establishment with no other uniqueness, it is critical that the skills in customer communications be used as guerrilla fighting tools.

Once the basic game plan (strategy) is identified, the retail establishment must plan the strategy implementation. This implementation is likely to make or break the retail establishment.

Strategy Implementation

Implementing the strategic plan is at least as important as having such a plan.

Four areas of consideration are identified as most critical in strategy implementation: retail mix combination, strategic business units (SBUs) versus profit centers (PCs), store product combinations, and personalizing efforts.

Retail Mix Combination

In chapter 2 five retail mixes are presented as the key strategic tools in retailing. These five mixes are presented in a reasonable but not exhaustive manner. Each one of these mixes plays a different role in the implementation of the seven strategic options discussed in this chapter.

- In broad terms, and general terms, a general merchandising strategy calls for a special emphasis on a goods and services mix (but mostly on goals).
- A general merchandise selection is the onus of this strategy. In recent years this mix has been combined with the pricing mix by the discounters who are doing extremely well at the writing of this book.
- In a differentiating strategy, the merchandise mix is still critical since it has to be somewhat different. But this difference must be communicated with the general market. Thus, the communication mix along with merchandise mix is important in this strategic orientation.
- A segmentation strategy may call for emphasis on a special merchandise and service mix. But this basic mix may have to have a pricing mix as a support function along with a communication mix to keep in touch with a well-defined target market.
- A positioning strategy is likely to emphasize all of the mixes almost equally because it is an all-out effort to put the store against typically a well-known, well-established competitor. It is a broader game plan that requires all of the nixes to come together and perform as needed to achieve the position a retailer may wish to reach and stay in the marketplace.
- A niching strategy would call for heavy emphasis on a goods and service mix, along with a human resource mix. The contact with a special corner of the market must be very close; therefore, the human resource mix plays a critical role in establishing a very close interaction with customers and maintaining that level of communication throughout. A logistics mix may have a special role in in-store considerations to make the store appealing and functional.
- A category killing strategy dwells, above all, upon a pricing mix. For the same variety, the retailer is offering much better prices and more attractive deals. The cost-cutting functions to support lower

prices are also critical; therefore, out-of-store logistics may be particularly critical.

• Guerrilla fighting calls for heavier emphasis on the human resource mix, since many different deals, with the customers, may be used to conduct business. Very specialized merchandise mix and communication mixes may be used to support the variety and creativity required to survive.

It must be realized that, in retailing, each retail store case is different and all mixes are important. They gave the retailer a reason for existence and made a contribution to the consumer's quality of life. This rather simplistic account of retail mixes vis-à-vis retail strategy implementation is just an attempt at consciousness raising. A retailer must be able to plan the implementation of the store's strategy by considering the relative roles of retail mixes. It must be understood that all retail mixes are important, but in our unique situation, some may be more important than others. Exhibit 8.2 presents a reasonably detailed account of the retail mixes. Again, individual retailers will have to add and delete some items to make these mixes more suitable for the particular needs of the store in question. It must be stated, however, that it is possible for a retailer to utilize more than one strategy. A category killer, for instance, can also be utilizing positioning strategy.

Implementing the retail strategic plan the second consideration is proper utilization of SBUs and PCs.

Utilizing SBUs and PCs

All stores must have SBUs. These are the outreach of the retail establishment. When a store is known by the quality of its workers or its convenience, these are SBUs. SBUs must make the store more recognizable so that customers will frequent the store. But when customers are frequenting the store, they must find something that is unique and of a good value; this brings the PCs into the picture. These unique and of good value products or services would create profit for the retail store. All products or services may not be profitable for the retail store. While some of them bring in customers, some products would create profit for the store. It is important to distinguish between the two groups of products and services. The relative roles and interaction between SBUs and PCs must be carefully assessed and understood. Unfortunately, these two concepts are commonly available in both marketing and accounting books; they are scarcely used in retailing practice. However, they could play a critical role in retailing for

Exhibit 8.2   Key Components of Retail Mixes

Goods and Services Mix	Communication Mix	Pricing Mix	Human Resource Mix	Logistics Mix
Merchandise	Advertising	Price Level	Personal Selling	Out-of-Store Logistics
Variety and Assortment	Catalogs	Price Lines	Customer Services	Contact and Coordination with Suppliers
Guarantee and Exchange	Store Layout	Markdowns	Interaction with Customers	
Customer Services	Public Relations	Markups	Merchandise Information	Resupply, Promotional Suppliers
Credit	Telephone Sales	Price/Perceived Quality	Salespeople's Advice	Deliver
Alterations and Adjustments	The Internet	Efficiency	Support People	External Warehousing
Delivery	Special Sales	Factors Affecting Prices	Maintenance	In-Source Logistics
Parking	Social Media	Warehouses	Cleaning	Inventory Control
		Handling Goods	Security	Merchandise Movement
		Computerized Controls	Delivery	Merchandise Location
			Satisfied Employees	Merchandise Combinations
				Internal Displays
				Window Displays
				Connection with Score Layout
Store Image	Store Image	Store Image	Store Image	Store Image

Source: Adapted and revised from Samli 2004.

strategy implementation. All retailers, regardless of size, have SBUs and PCs. Both SBUs and PCs are comprised of groups of products or, in some cases, departments that have a common market base.

If there are managers of some of these special units, they typically have complete responsibility to integrate all of their function into the retailing strategy to fulfill certain goals to compete with readily iden-tifiable competitors (Samli 2004). The manager of the sporting goods department in Walmart is certainly competing with similar depart-ments in other discount department stores as well as with sporting goods stores (Samli and Shaw 2002).

SBUs are very important in establishing a competitive advantage for a retail store because they are the outreach of the store. It is possible, for instance, that while a seafood market is known for the freshness of its products, a competitor may be well known for only its lobster prices. Similarly, one supermarket may be very well known for its deli center, whereas another is well known for its fresh produce center. These unique departments or product groups increase the stores out-side reach and enhance its image. As a result, the store attracts more customers because of its increasing market outreach.

PCs, on the other hand, imply internal strength of the retail estab-lishment. When the customers come in, they buy products from the PCs, and these, in return, make a greater contribution to the profit picture. However, the critical issue here is that while some products or departments have more external or market appeal, others bring more money in. But, quite often, if not most of the time, retail management may not make a distinction between the two. Clearly, it is very critical to distinguish SBUs from PCs and decide the external strengths and the internal strengths of the store and how they could be balanced. Exhibit 8.3 illustrates interconnections between SBUs and PCs. As displayed in the exhibit the upper-left quadrant depicts the optimal situation. When certain product groups or departments are both care-fully selected as SBUs and PCs, the store is at an optimal level. Both SBUs and PC are chosen well and they are reasonably balanced in creating internal and external appeals. This also means that SBUs and PCs are synergistic optimizing the retail store's performance. The opposite, of course, is the lower-right quadrant. The retailer, in this situation, does not know the store's internal and external strengths. As a result, no distinction is made between SBUs and PCs. The end result in such situations, which this author believes are not uncom-mon, is likely to be the end of the retail establishment in question. In the lower-left quadrant, if the retailer survives and makes money it certainly will not be in the short run. Putting a lot of emphasis for the store's outreach but not enough attractive merchandise (PCs) inter-nally makes it difficult for the store to make progression. As stated earlier, PCs and SBUs must both be present and paid attention to. On the other hand, the upper-right quadrant is a short-run story. The retail establishment has good PCs but this is almost a well-kept secret.

Exhibit 8.3 The Interaction between SBUs and PCs

Strategic Business Units

	Good Choice	Poor Choice
Good Choice	Good management Balancing the internal and external appeals	Questionable management Toomany internal and too few external appeals
Profit Centers		
Poor Choice	Borderline poor management Managing too many external and too few internal appeals	Poor management Managing too few and ineffective internal and external appeals

Source: Adapted and revised from Samli (2004).

The store does not have external market power to bring customers in. If the customers are not coming in, they cannot patronize the store and buy products which may be used as PCs. As can be seen, in implementing the retail strategic plan successfully, it is critical for the retailer to have the PCs and SBUs identified and well balanced. Consider the following: an independent department store in a southeast university town has had a very busy small restaurant. One day the management shut it down. The reason was that the restaurant "was not yielding any profits." The department store management had never analyzed what the restaurant customers bought before and after eating. Thus, the restaurant which was a SBU was eliminated without anyone assessing its contribution to the store's PCs (Samli and Shaw 2002). On a smaller scale, retailing PCs and SBUs may not be totally separate departments but only separate product groups.

Store-Product Combinations

A retailer must know the limits of that store's product concentration. In typical marketing courses, three groups of product categories— convenience goods, shopping goods, and specialty goods—are mentioned. Similarly, this author believes that there are retailers emphasizing convenience goods such as Seven Elevens, or shopping goods as most department stores are, or specialty goods such as Tiffany's. The important point here is that convenience goods stores, shopping goods stores, and specialty goods stores must concentrate on convenience products, shopping products, and specialty products, respectively. If

Gate's convenience stores start offering Rolex watches or Sears start selling very expensive diamonds, or Tiffany's offer disposable diapers, these situations not only create confusion but make it so that consumers may not know exactly what they will buy where.

While the convenience stores such as ice cream parlors, sandwich shops, or household necessitate offering convenience stores deal with basic needs; on the other hand shopping stores such as Target or Sears offer a variety of consumer durables, from furniture to apparel and more; finally, specialty stores such as upscale jewelry stores, apparel stores, or upscale department stores such as Neiman Marcus must concentrate on the products and services they meant to offer, but they should not deviate from offering the key product categories they originally meant to offer.

Personalizing Efforts

Discounting retail giants have millions of customers by using the modern electronic data-generating techniques, they are developing big data. Big data is a concept dealing with the data sets that are too large and too complex for conventional data-processing applications. It is stated that utilizing this kind of data is important for some retailers to gain an advantage in their markets (Biesdorf, Court, and Wilmott 2013).

From a retailing perspective, big data can provide specific information about retailing customers for pre-purchase, purchase, and post-purchase situations.

Pre-purchase information: Reams of data flow which indicate where the customers are, who the regulars are, what are they likely to buy, and what would be proper promotion and other offerings to bring them into the store or participate online (McAfee and Brynjolfson2013). If the retailer can collect, integrate, and analyze these data, it is assumed that it will do better than average in the market (Brown, Chui, and Manyika 2012).

Purchase information: Understanding how the customer travels across the store, identifying database of point of sale (POS) and point of payments (PPs) are critical components of big data. All of these can be analyzed in such a way that the retailer will be able to direct in-store activity in detail.

Post-purchase information: Many messages in the big media are related to contacting customers to avoid buyer's remorse as well as reinforcing possible feeling of satisfaction from recent purchases.

Of those who are using big data, the retail giants would utilize and particularly benefit from pre- and post-purchase information. Although they do have purchase information as well, they have such large number of customers that the utilization and some way of application of purchase information are rather difficult for the retail giants. This is where the small and medium-sized independent retailers can generate some advantage. Since the purchase information deals with individual customer's behavior during the purchase behavior in store, the smaller independents can use that information for personalization. This portion of the total big data is coined here as *small data*.

Small Data

The advancement of information technology (IT) has provided consumers with mobile communication devices while giving retailers sensor networks, among other information exchange devices, which are creating information-gathering possibilities. The small and medium-sized retailers can use these data to make their customers more comfortable and more satisfied than discounting giants could. In the modern retail establishments when a purchase is made, it is automatically registered as to how much was paid for it. Furthermore, customer's choice of paying cash versus paying by credit card is automatically registered indicating perhaps the preferred price range. Another customer motivation is negotiation on price. While most small and medium-sized independents don't directly compete on price, they can illustrate some examples of good prices based on the existing local competition. Retailers are also exploring how advanced mobile phones can be used at the point of sale (POS) system in the store by the customers themselves. Additionally, most POS systems have the ability to uniquely identify a customer, using either a frequent shopping card, phone number, or other similar attributes. When combined with the POS information, the system is also able to store a series of customer preferences such as what they mainly buy in that store, how much, and how often.

Small and medium-sized retailers who are concentration on small data can generate types of information to serve their customers better. Exhibit 8.4 presents five different small data information and specifies how they are used to improve their customers' shopping experience.

In chapter 6, ten shopping motives are discussed. Small data would contribute to five of these. Exhibit 8.5 illustrates how small data would make a contribution to enhancing shopping motives (Samli and Gupta 2014). As can be seen, small data, if gathered and used properly, would make an important contribution to the independent smaller-scale retailers to personalize retailing experiences.

Exhibit 8.4   Electronic Information in Small Data

Type of Information	Decisions Based on Information
Detecting shopping patterns	Developing a good merchandise mix
Evaluating customer priorities	Inventory control, more promotion
Learning what they pay cash for	Making customer friendly pricing decision
In general what do they move	Making these products more available
Physical examination	Rearranging store layout instructing sales people

Source: Adapted and revised from Samli and Gupta 2014.

Exhibit 8.5   Small Data Contribution to Shopping Motives

Shopping Motive	Meaning	Small Data Contribution
Learning More	New fashions, popular styles, etc.	Providing this information to customers
Sensory Stimulation	Interacting with products more closely	Giving more information about average products
Negotiation	Being able to compare contrast before purchase	Sharing information about pricing in the store and competitors' prices
Satisfying Needs and Wants	Choosing from and buying of variety of products	Identifying the preferences and reiterating them
Satisfying Shopping Needs	Being able to shop efficiently and leisurely	Making the store a comfortable place to shop leisurely

Source: Adapted and revised from Samli and Gupta 2014.

Utilizing Human Senses

In personalizing the retailing experience for the consumer by using small data, it is quite appropriate for small or medium-sized retailers who cannot be discounter, but they can give more value to their customers. Here, making a trip to the retail store more pleasurable can be achieved not only by providing the favorite product mix conveniently, making shopping and buying in store easier, and providing a pleasant atmosphere are good approaches for the nonretailing giants to level the playing field, but adding the enhancement of human senses for the customer will make an important addition to small-scale independents. This is the area where retail giants cannot make much progress because of their millions of customers who go for large variety and discounts. Human sense experiences dealing with hearing, touching, smelling, seeing, and tasting are real, and retailers that are trying to

Exhibit 8.6   Combining Small Data and Sensory Touch

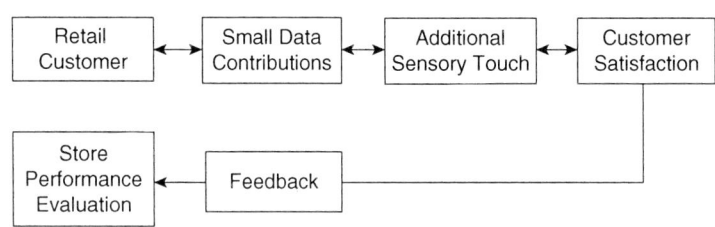

Source: Adapted and revised from Samli and Gupta 2014.

individualize the shopping experiences for their customers can use scent, music, design, taste, and texture to enhance the sensory experiences of their customers for greater satisfaction (Hulten, Browers, and VanDijk 2009). Some of the sensory experiences have been used over the years sporadically, such as small restaurants, department stores, new car smells by auto makers, and baked goods section of supermarkets, but they have not been systematically organized as part of the retailing strategies. Human senses can be used by smaller independents to personalize their customers' experiences. Small data can be developed and used for this purpose.

Exhibit 8.6 presents the total position of personalization of retail experiences which is what smaller independents must dwell upon. This is one important way of gaining an edge over discounters.

SUMMARY

In order to cater effectively to the chosen targets the smaller independents must develop a strategic plan. It must be understood that there are segment modifiers to which independent retailers must adjust.

Seven key strategy options identified and discussed in this chapter. They are examined in the form of retail mix combinations.

But the most important aspect of the chapter lies on the four different activities to implement the strategies. The first activity is, which retail mixes are actually used in the strategy implementation. The second activity is identifying SBUs and PCs and using them properly. Third, store-product combinations and their importance are discussed. But, the most important aspect of the chapter is a brief and to the point presentation of small data. This is where smaller independents can make their mark and gain an edge over discounters.

9

DEVELOPING, MEASURING, AND MANAGING STORE IMAGE

A consumer entering Sam's or Costco certainly experiences different feelings from one entering Neiman Marcus or Saks Fifth avenue. These feelings will be accentuated by ambiance, merchandise, service, and other store features (Samli 2004). Every retail store has a person ality that is the sum total of impressions a consumer will experience as he/she enters the store and shops around. That atmosphere, which is called store image, may be very suitable for some customers, and totally unsuitable for others.

Individuals do not face a new stimulus such as exploring a new store as if this was a completely novel experience. This idea is developed and promoted by the category-based processing theory which implies that a variety of experiential information modified the intensity of the current experience and expectation (Samli 2004). Consumers will compare incoming information against the knowledge and/or experiences that they have stored in their memories. This means, for instance, if the consumer is going to a new restaurant for the first time, that consumer has some expectations based on previous experiences. The same thing is true for going to, say, a supermarket for the first time or patronizing an apparel store for the first time. For the new small-scale independent retailer this means not simply promoting newness or uniqueness of the store but also connecting this new store to consumers' typical and general experiences. This is partly starting to develop a store image for the new store.

Exhibit 9.1 illustrates how this theory works in reality. An individual who is familiar with Walmart encounters a new Walmart unit. The information imparted by the new Walmart store in the form of promotion, ambiance, service, and so forth comes into play in comparison with past experiences with Walmart.

Exhibit 9.1 Encountering and Perceiving a Store Image

Step

1. The store must match a previously defined category of stores. (Oh! Here is the new Walmart Store. I wonder how it compares to the other Walmart's. I have seen.)

2. The store must give out cues that will match information about the category of store it belongs to. (The consumer enters. Well! It seems like just about the same merchandise and the same layout.)

3. If the store is perceived to match an existing category of stores, it means it activated the criteria to describe that category. (I wonder if this Walmart is better in giving out information than others, so we can compare.)

4. If the set of criteria is activated, all the information is transferred to this store. (It appears that the salespeople here don't know much about consumer electronics, just as the others.)

5. If the set of criteria is activated, this set will determine the relevance and consistency of the information about the store. (Gee! This Walmart is exactly the same as the others. I have had good experiences with Walmart's before.)

A retail store is not only a place where goods and services are purchased. It is also a place where a combination of functional and emotional stimuli is perceived. Much of this orientation is presented in chapter 8. It must be reiterated that these functional and emotional stimuli which are emitted by every retail establishment make or break that store. It is extremely important to understand that the total sum of these stimuli is the store image (Samli 2004). Throughout that store image, a retail store communicates many personal and impersonal aspects that distinguish it from other stores. Each and every store, intentionally or unintentionally, emits many tangible and intangible stimuli that are synergistic. Thus, a retail store's functional qualities, physical attributes, its atmosphere, and many other symbolic characteristics are all intertwined in the form of a store image.

EVERY STORE HAS AN IMAGE

No retail establishment is all things to all people. As a store continues to perform, even if it has not done so deliberately, it will develop an image de facto. It is critical to realize that an image projected deliberately is always better than an image emerging after the fact. In deliberate attempts, the retailer is being proactive rather than reactive or inactive. As the store promotes its functional qualities and psychological attributes, it is projecting a synergistic image that would reflect its differential congruence. The functional qualities are related to how well the store meets the aspirations of its target market by providing price, quality, product mix, service, and store logistics.

The store's psychological attributes are less tangible and more difficult to evaluate. Appealing to the psyche and sensory perceptions of consumers is extremely difficult, and the measurement of this appeal is even more difficult but every store must make an attempt to assess the store's overall perception by consumers.

A store, however, must be realistic and perhaps a little subtle as it makes deliberate statements such as:

- this is the place where shopping is absolute pleasure;
- this is the friendliest place you have ever shopped;
- we have the best value given to you by the most reasonable prices; and
- this is the ultimate destination for lingerie.

By definition, the image is projected and communicated through personal and impersonal communications in the form of a combination of tangible and intangible characteristics that provide an overall symbolic impression. The latter says, "Hey! This is what I am." Of course, if the store's claims and the customers' perceptions of the store do not match, then there is no possibility of creating differential congruence, which again is the essence of the store's competitive advantage.

In many ways strategic retailing can be described as developing and managing a store's image. Because store image is such a complex and synergistic phenomenon, the retailer must thoroughly master the concept. Certainly, an ineffective and inadequate store image management activity is not likely to enhance the retailer's chances for survival.

Dimensions of Store Image

The store image is a combination of many tangible and intangible features that emanates from the store. If a retailer is to use store image as a key strategic weapon to achieve competitive advantage, the key components of store image must be known and prioritized. Thus the store image can be used to best advantage. The key point here is that the retailer must know what components are most important and how they are likely to be promoted.

Exhibit 9.2 illustrates nine dimensions of store image. These dimensions carry different weights, depending on the choice of

Exhibit 9.2   The Key Dimensions of a Store Image

Dimension	Description
Merchandise MIX	There are at least five identifiable subdimensions: quality, selection or assortment, styling or fashion, guarantees, and pricing.
Service	The areas included in this dimension are: general service, salesclerk service, presence of self-service, ease of merchandise return, delivery service, and credit policies.
Clientele	Just who buys in the store and how loyal are they
Physical Facilities	The features included here are: elevators, lighting, air conditioning, washrooms, along with store layout, aisle placement, section identification, carpeting, and architecture.
Convenience	Three key subdimensions are identified: general convenience, location convenience, and parking.
Promotion	This group includes sales promotion, advertising, displays, coupons, symbols, and colors.
Store Atmosphere	This is an intangible category. Included are congeniality, customers' feelings, and ambience.
Institutional Factors	This is also an intangible category. It deals with reliability, reputation, and modernity.
Post transaction Satisfaction	Included here are merchandise in use, returns and adjustments, receptiveness to complaints and other desires.

Source: Adapted and revised from Samli 2004.

strategy and the way it is implemented by the retail establishment. A category killer, for instance, would emphasize the first dimension reported in the exhibit, which encompasses merchandise and pricing of the merchandise. However, a differentiator may find it more effective to promote and use the store atmosphere. If the store is positioned above the competitor's price range, it may emphasize all the physical aspects of the image and use more psychological dimensions of the image.

Images vary not only by store type but also from one market segment to another. The retailer, obviously, must be able to understand, evaluate, and use the key image dimensions so that a synergistic and effective image can be construed and, if necessary, manipulated. All of these activities dwell upon measuring the current store image and adjusting, if needed, to current trends, events, and other forces that influence the store's image.

Image Measurement

In order to manage the image, it is critical that it is accurately assessed. Different techniques can be used to measure the store image; however, once the store image is measured in a specific way, then it must be continued to be measured in the same way so that there will be continuity of measurement, so as to reveal any expected or unexpected changes.

Exhibit 9.3 presents some important techniques used in store image measurement. Two groups of measurement techniques are used for this purpose, unstructured and structured.

Unstructured Measurement Techniques

Four such techniques are presented in the Exhibit 9.3. Word association is an old and widely used psychological technique. Free word association deals with what comes to mind first as the particular store is mentioned. This could be rather serious if the responding customers say derogatory things about the store.

Sentence completion is used by marketing researchers also quite often. Completing the sentence presents the whole thought process

Exhibit 9.3 Store Image Measurement

Techniques (Unstructured)	Description
Word Association	Trying to determine which word comes to mind in describing the store
Sentence Completion	If I want to get the best value for the price I will go to…
Cartoon Test	Describe the customers that you see in the picture and what they are doing.
Open-Ended Questions	What do you like the most about shopping at XYZ Store?

Techniques (Structured)	Description
Semantic Differential	Locate us on the continuum: Modern ↔ Old fashioned
Multidimensional Scaling	Comparing stores on a perceptual map
Multiattribute Models	Semantic differential with weights to establish relative importance of each factor
Multivariate Techniques	Highly quantitative, sophisticated techniques including clustering, discriminant analysis, factor analysis, and canonical analysis.

that reflects the individual's thinking about the store. Consider, for instance, an incomplete sentence such as when I shop here…The respondent could have many alternatives to finish the sentence.

The cartoon test is not as commonly used as it should be. It can bring up deeper impressions about the store. How the test is designed and how it is interpreted are critical points in using this technique.

Open-ended questions are very practical and quite commonly used to obtain free thinking about the store. Asking respondents about their impressions of the store and receiving their comments in their own words is an effective way of determining how the store image works. The analysis of results of this test may be rather difficult, however, since there may be many varying opinions about the store. A psychologist's interpretive skills may be needed.

Structured Techniques

The difference between "structured" and "unstructured" techniques is the form of response. Whereas in unstructured techniques, the response is not formatted, and respondents can use their own approach for answers and verbal expressions, in the structured techniques, the response is formatted. This means that they are oriented more toward attitudinal orientation which would be displayed by choosing one of the few alternatives as the response to the question. In that sense it may be stated that while structured techniques may have a tendency to measure attitudes, unstructured techniques may help to identify motives that influence the customers to patronize the store. These motives in some cases deal with subconscious aspects of purchase behavior and may shed light on new and unexpected dimensions about the store that management may not have thought previously. In one such study, for instance, researchers discovered that some consumers considered the store to be an easy place for shoplifting. That could not have been measured by structured techniques.

Four structured techniques are identified in Exhibit 9.3.

Semantic differential: Of the four structured techniques that are listed in Exhibit 9.3, the semantic differential is the most commonly used one. Marketing scholars have traditionally used the semantic differential technique for different aspects of store image analysis. For instance, it has been used for measuring the impact of television advertising on store image, or to determine the differences between symbolic and functional store images among many other important ones used (Samli 1998).

The technique is easy to administer and tabulate. It also allows the presentation of the processed data in a format that is easily understood and visually formatted. It does not require extensive verbal skills on the part of the respondents. They can respond rather easily. Additionally, the technique is considered to be quite reliable in the sense that the results are consistent under typical and similar conditions.

However, two problem areas are related to the semantic differential. First, the research needs to determine the attributes (or characteristics) of the store to be included in the measurement instrument. Second, we must assess the relative importance of these attributes and how they are related to each other, that is, to what extent these store characteristics are interrelated and how they contribute to the overall store image (Samli 2004).

Multidimensional Scaling

Multidimensional scaling (MDS) is a newer and a more sophisticated tool that is used to measure store image. It also is versatile enough to be used in different aspects of store image measurements. MDS makes the fewest possible assumptions regarding the respondent's reactions. Furthermore, it provides the respondent to making the fewest possible judgments. As a result of these special features in using MDS, respondents can be objective in a very subjective attitudinal questioning process. The process can help management evaluate the store's image in comparison with a competitor's image. This is not a very simple technique to administer and analyze, however.

Multiattribute models: These models attempt to rectify the major deficiencies in the semantic differential method. In the semantic differential, all of the variables are given the same weight. What if, for example, in the case of Store A, location is not as important as the merchandise mix or price mix? The semantic differential fails to point out this very important bit of information, but a multiattribute model will.

Marketers have been using this technique since it was developed by Fishbein in 1967. The technique enables the researcher to determine which store attributes are particularly important (Saliance) and their respective degrees of importance (Valence). As a result, multiattribute models accomplish more than the semantic differential. However, this technique also has the same problems that the semantic differential has; as discussed above, since there are some major variations in the application of the technique, and since there are many attributes that can be used, which variables or dimensions must be used becomes a critical issue.

Multivariate techniques: A variety of techniques fit under this title (Samli 1996). They are all geared for different types of analyses of the same phenomenon. The description of each technique is beyond the scope of this book. However, it can be simply stated that clustering can, for instance, profile loyal customers of the store, which is an indirect way of measuring the store image. Discriminant analysis can distinguish the characteristics of the key specific features of two competing stores. Factor analysis identifies whether there are certain hidden factors that might influence store loyalty, and canonical analysis verifies, for example, the presence of multiple store image definitions and their important components. Even though these are quite powerful techniques, they have not been used extensively in retailing research (Samli 2004).

Managing the Image

Measuring the store's image is important only if it leads to managing the store image well. A well-managed store image, by definition, enhances the profitability and success. However, that implies the store image measurement has generated a better-managed store image. This

Exhibit 9.4   Store Image Management Paradigm

Steps	Functions
Step 1 Evaluate the current store image	• Define the store image • Identify its important dimensions and their respective importance • Measure the current image according to the first two functions
Step 3 Determine the changes to be made in the current image	• Identify the store's strengths and weaknesses • Decide where changes need to take place • Compare the desired changes and the expected direction of the store
Step 4 Implement and evaluate the changes that have been introduced	• Identify specifically each change that has been implemented • Evaluate the impact of these changes vis-à-vis the key competitor • Critically decide if the new changes should continue
Step 5 Relate the image changes to the store performance	• Measure the changes in sales and market share • Remeasure customers' store loyalty • Contrast the changes between loyal customers and new customers • Evaluate changes in profitability

would lead to increased sales and profitability. The retailer's repeat business is a major strength, and is a function of a well-managed store image. Additionally, the store image works with product or brand image in a synergistic manner creating additional value to the product as well as the store. Studies have shown that products in an upscale store have a more favorable image than the same products in a lower-scale store. Other studies have indicated that store image is used by consumers as a method of risk reduction. If the consumers believe in the store where they are shopping, then they feel more confident about the product (Samli 2004).

From our discussion thus far, it is clear that the retailer must have a proactive approach to constructing and managing the store's image. Exhibit 9.4 presents a five-step image management model. These five steps are the following: evaluate the current store image, establish a reference point, determine the changes to be made in the current image, implement and evaluate the changes that have been introduced, and relate the image changes to the store's performance.

A floor-covering store (selling carpeting, rugs, and other such supplies) tried to find out if it should go more heavily into discounting. Following the five steps led to these conclusions:

- The current store image indicated that it was respected as a "classy" place.
- Its key competitor is a discounter clearly appealing to a different group of clientele.
- The store decided to play up its classy status.
- As a classy store it provided more advice for interior decoration and a slightly higher quality merchandise mix.
- The store found out the reinforcement of its current image worked well and it stayed away from discounting.

Evaluating the Current Store Image

If we don't know what consumers think about us in the market, how can we improve our image? Understanding the current image begins with its perception by our customers. This perception may indicate other features about our store are in existence but we did not know them until now. These new features that we discovered need to be evaluated as to their importance and their role in the overall store image. If it was decided upon that these newly discovered features are rather important for our store, they may be emphasized readily in the revised store image projection. It is quite possible that by using the multiattribute analysis, the retailer may find that the employee's knowledge level is much more critical than the store's price level policy. This, of course, is almost essential for small-scale independents. If small-scale independents are emphasizing personalizing efforts as discussed in chapter 8, then the employee's attitude and knowledge base become extremely critical. The retailer, therefore, has the option of keeping this feature as it is, strengthening it by providing more training for the employees, or promoting this feature more readily, to mention just a few courses of action.

Establishing a Reference Point

The decisions relating to which image dimensions to keep and which ones to modify will be partially dependent on the reference points that are established. The reference points can be established by evaluating the image of a key competitor. Once the competitor's strengths are identified and their relative importance for the store's image is approximated, then it becomes rather important for our retailer to decide if we want to be a deviator, imitator, complementer, or innovator (see chapter 2) vis-à-vis this competition.

Determining the Changes to be Made

Based on the above two steps, it is possible to decide on the store's strengths and weaknesses. It is critical here to decide what (if any) changes must be implemented in reconstructing and projecting the store's image. Clearly, the changes implemented in the store image are likely to take the store in an expected and/or hoped for direction. Of course, the research may show that the store is very strong in its target markets. Hence, rather than changing or slightly modifying the current image, reinforcing it may be the best alternative. This implies that the store is emphasizing its proper and well-accepted strengths. These existing image features are more effective than other alternatives.

Implement and Evaluate

After a retailer comes to understand the store's weaknesses and strengths and decide what changes in the image are likely to be initiated, implementation becomes critical.

The difference between the previous image and the currently revised image needs to be carefully examined. Here image-related research data are necessary. The store may be able to conduct a before/after analysis. In such analysis, it is critical that these two sets of data be comparable. In order for the two sets of data to be comparable, the data collection techniques, data collection instruments, and data analysis methodology must be totally identical.

Once the previous image and the new image are compared, the constraints of validity and reliability of the data gathered become critical. It should become obvious that the attempts to improve the image have been successful. As the previous and the new images are compared, it must be evident that the current image is succeeding in the direction that the changes were intended to accomplish. For instance, customers indicated that a better store layout was much desired. However, if after the new store layout introduced the reaction is that the new layout is not even as good as the old one, then the difference is not in the direction that was intended. It is clear that the direction and the intensity of the changes as a result of the implemented new strategy must be quickly and accurately measured.

Relate Image Changes to the Performance

The changes in the new store image must be reflected in the store's performance; otherwise the store is simply wasting time, effort, and resources. Thus, the success of the four steps in Exhibit 9.4 can only be realistically determined from the fifth step. The market performance of the retail store is the ultimate measure of store image management. There are at least four different ways to measure the store's market performance. First, changes in sales volume and market share can be measured and compared with the same period in the past. Second, the change in the degree of store loyalty displayed by the customers can be evaluated. Are the same customers coming to the store regularly easily determined? Third, the store outreach is assessed by examining if the store is attracting customers from further distances. And finally, the profitability of the store can be utilized as the key criterion of performance evaluation. It is clear that the market performance is improving if the improvements in the image are bringing in more profits. Going back to an earlier theme, differential congruence is being reinforced and further strengthened if the image management effort is working well.

DIFFERENTIAL CONGRUENCE ONCE AGAIN

As we develop and manage the store image, we must make sure that it is acceptable to our target market. This is how differential congruence is developed and strengthened. Differential congruence gives viability to a retail establishment and reinforces its probability of success. In order to achieve differential congruence, a harmony between the store image and the individual customers' self-image is required. Through its efforts to project a store image, the retailer claims the presence of certain features that are unique to the store, which then differentiates it from other competing retail establishments. Above all, these store features are consistent with the store customers' self-image. The congruence between these two images leads to greater long-term customer satisfaction and resultant customer loyalty. The value derived from patronizing the retail establishment translates into profit for the retailer.

It is critical to reiterate that the store image is a product of the store's functional and psychological (emotional) features. These two groups of features lead to a symbolic store image. Early research studies mostly concentrated on the store's functional features. We see, then, a gap in research findings relating to a store's emotional (psychological) features and resultant symbolic features that comprise the total store personality.

The symbolic, value-expressive store image deals with generalities such as traditional versus modern, high status versus low status, pleasant atmosphere versus not so pleasant atmosphere, and the like. If a customer perceives that on the basis of its functional and psychological features, a store is patronized by primarily high-class customers and that person sees himself as a high-class customer and that person also sees himself as a high-class consumer, then there will be congruence as intended, and that customer is likely to develop store loyalty. Needless to say, store loyalty means repeat sales and repeat sales make a difference between surviving and not surviving in retailing. Creating such a congruence with its customers in its trading area indicates that the store is making a reasonable contribution to its customers' quality of life which is the essence of differential advantage. In its customers' minds the store is different from others, and shopping there is a pleasant experience because the store has a symbolic image that is very consistent with the individual customer's own self-image.

WHEN MANAGEMENT AND CUSTOMERS PERCEIVE THINGS DIFFERENTLY

In trying to establish congruence, analyzing customer's perceptions of the store image compared to management's perception of the store image can be an important diagnostic tool.

Such analysis may indicate, for instance, that customers think the store is not modern, whereas management thinks it is; similarly, customers may think that store's personnel are not at all friendly, and the management thinks the personnel are exceptionally good and so on. Based on such discrepancies, Exhibit 9.5 is constructed.

The upper-left quadrant illustrates a rather idealistic situation. Both the management and customers think the store is outstanding. This situation may even identify certain special strengths of the store that were not noticed before. These special strengths can be further used in the future to promote the store and create a stronger congruence.

The upper-right quadrant is a critical problem situation. It appears that neither customers nor the store management are happy with the current conditions. But since both groups are in agreement, this situation can be remedied. Negative congruence of this type if detected quickly can be corrected to both parties satisfaction. The lower-right quadrant of Exhibit 9.5 indicates that a number of problems undetected earlier have surfaced and needed to be taken care of. But these problems are either different types or are perceived differently by the management and customers. While both groups realize the store has serious problems, they disagree on what these problems are. This is a very difficult situation. It may not be corrected effectively.

Finally, the lower-left quadrant indicates that the store has many positive features, but, again, management and customers disagree as to what these positive features are. If the store continues this way, it can maintain its existence but it certainly is missing possible profits and stronger congruence.

Exhibit 9.5 Discrepancy between Management and Customer Perception

	Positive Aspects of the Store	Negative Aspects of the Store
Management and Customers Agree	Indicating the true strengths of the store	There are clear-cut weaknesses of the store and these can be corrected.
Management and Customers Disagree	Unknown strengths of the store may emerge. Management may be wrong in its thinking.	There are a number of unnoticed weaknesses. The disagreement by two groups makes these weaknesses uneasy to correct.

Source: Adapted and revised from Samli 2004.

An Illustration

Upon an analysis of customers' and management's evaluation of the store's performance, a small gift shop adjacent to a major university in a small southeastern town realized that it belonged in the lower-right quadrant of Exhibit 9.5. Analysis indicated that one store has limited variety, limited stock for the products it offered, and a confusing atmosphere because the store was run by part-time help who did not know how to organize the store and its inventory. The management thought it was its promotional efforts which were not reaching the right market segment. Management laid out a series of strategic alternatives:

• Have more and better-trained full-time staff to help serve customers with more appealing merchandise mix. Cater to students more by making the store more student friendly.
• Make the store more nonstudent oriented. Change the store image somewhat, adjust the merchandise mix accordingly, and appeal to young adults in town.
• Develop the store and its atmosphere to appeal to the upper middle class, with significantly improved ambience, merchandise mix, and general orientation. Establishing a name outside of town to attract more out of owners.

Although all three strategic alternatives appeared to be attractive, the first one seemed to be more doable with less risk, since the university is growing and students have more discretionary income. It also appeared that since the current target market consists of students, alternatives 2 and 3 would not create differential congruence and move the store from the lower-right quadrant to the upper-left quadrant in Exhibit 9.5.

Implementing alternatives, however, was not as simple as it may seem. There are many details to take care of which are likely to strengthen the store further in its niching strategy. The management pondered the possibility of expanding the merchandise mix more in the direction of coeds, developing more liberal return policy and implementing certain tactics of grouping the new merchandise in a dorm-room arrangement, and displaying the most attractive new lines in the best possible manner. Such a proactive approach to differential congruence development is bound to get some positive results. Of course, the management should have contingency plans in case the new strategy implementation does not work as well as expected.

All Must End Up in Store Loyalty

As has been reiterated a few times in retailing, we are selling a store image. If that image is consistent with the self-image of the consumers in the store's target market, the store has a good chance to succeed. Here the retailer must identify the characteristics of the target market's behavior patterns and must make sure that they are all considered when an attempt is made to promote the store.

It is clear that store loyalty implies the existence of differential congruence. The store management must be able to assess if there is store loyalty and if there is by whom. The indicators of store loyalty are as follows:

- When it is detected that some customers visit the store often.
- If those customers do not shop around much before coming to our store.
- They buy most, if not all, of what they need in our store.
- If the customers display a preference for our store by choosing it on every possible occasion.
- The customers have definite intention to come back to our store.
- When the customers recommend our store to others.

It is obvious that the points made in this chapter require up-front information as well as follow-up information in the form of feedback. As indicated in Chapter 8, small scale independents can and should generate small data that retail giants do not or cannot generate. It is also strongly posited that in small scale retailing being engaged in understanding individual customers and catering to their needs is their essence. It must also be posited that the management of small scale independents understand and use research. Being able to conduct and use small data is related to research skills and how to use research findings.

Summary

This is a critical chapter for, particularly, small-scale independent retailers. They must understand that the sum total of all the impressions emanating from a store is what the store image is. Whether it is intentional or not, all retail establishments have an image. By making it deliberate or intentional is the critical function of good management. It is pointed out in this chapter that the store image has multiple dimensions. Nine such dimensions are discussed in this chapter.

The techniques used to measure store image are briefly discussed in the chapter. It is critical that the retail managers understand its importance and measure the store's image. The measurement techniques are categorized into two groups: unstructured and structured. At times, using more than one technique may be necessary.

A five-step store image management process is presented in the chapter. This process allows, in fact at times necessitates, and changes to be made in the existing image of the store. It is reiterated in the chapter that image management creates differential congruence. Successful differential congruence reflects customer loyalty. There are multiple approaches to measure store loyalty. The retailer must be able to conduct and use research, once again, for all of the important objectives that are laid out in this chapter.

10

PEOPLE ARE OUR STRENGTH

Retailing is people business as such; it cannot be managed by clichés and dogmas. All that is being said is "people are the key cost in your business, keep that cost low." Would paying low salaries and replacing the employees with cheaper labor be really profitable? Discounting giants may think so or they simply don't care. Small independent retailers must consider their people a major asset rather than a key liability.

What if a retailer were to treat its workers well by paying them reasonable wages, providing health care, giving promotions regularly, and the like? That retail establishment would have satisfied workers who are loyal, enthusiastic, excited about their work, and extremely customer friendly. In chapter 9 we presented a possibility that personalizing their customers is one of the major possibilities for independent small scalars to gain an edge over discounters. Certainly personalizing customers would not work if the store's personnel are not happy and the turnover rate of the store's employees is very high.

A satisfied and reasonably happy retail employee is loyal to the store, determined to do well, enthusiastic, and clearly very customer oriented. If and when the retail workers are leaving because they are unhappy or being replaced by the retailer in favor of cheaper labor, the above-mentioned positive attitudes and the resultant good performance do not exist.

A not carefully analyzed aspect of retail personnel issues is the cost of high employee turnovers. It is not quite well understood that there are direct and indirect cost of high turnover rate and/or the behavior of dissatisfied personnel. These would create dysfunctional personnel.

DYSFUNCTIONAL PERSONNEL

It must be reiterated that the discounting giants do not pay much attention to the interaction between the personnel and customers since that interaction is very minimal and inconsequential. However, for small-scale independent this is a major strategy. They have to have well-functioning personnel that would make the customers comfortable. However, most small-scale independents deal mostly with minimum cost for personnel and they miss the opportunity to establish very strong customer relations. They end up having dysfunctional personnel. Some of the key aspects of this dysfunctionality are presented in Exhibit 10.1.

Somehow it is not quite understood or appreciated that replacing a worker is recruitment. If done properly, which means finding a good person who would do the job well, it will cost time and effort. This time and effort is never accounted for. This author knows of a mid-size independent retail complex that had almost 100 percent turnover rate. The owner-manger spent tremendous amounts of time arguing with firing of and recruiting workers. The situation got so bad that the owner-manager did not do anything about strategy development, plans for improvement, and general management. The end result is that, at the writing of this book, the business is in bankruptcy. Particularly, the recruiting activity takes much time, and that is costly; hence, hiring and keeping good people would save much money.

Regardless of how complicated or how simple the retailing job is, all retailing jobs must be based on some careful training. Consider the following situation:

Mr. A went to his corner branch of the national bank where he conducted his financial businesses for many years. Very recently the bank has been getting new people who were creating puzzling situations. That particular day Mr. A was depositing some money in his checking account. Two new people asked him if he had his ID. When Mr. A asked what for, they responded "anybody can make a deposit."

Exhibit 10.1   Impact of Dysfunctional Personnel

Direct Cost Factors
- Recruiting cost
- Cost of training
- Developmental expenses

Indirect Cost Factors
- Poor treatment of customers
- Lack of interest in doing the job well
- Excessive sick leaves
- Unhappy workers searching another job

Mr. A responded saying that he has never been asked for an ID during the past 20 years. Another person in the bank suggested that she knew Mr. A when a deposit slip with a balance came out, the amount deposited and available amount indicated for transactions were the same and did not include the thousands of dollars deposited that day. When Mr. A asked for an explanation, the response was: these checks have not been cashed yet. They may not be good. In balance there always have been a difference with what was deposited and what is available for use. Mr. A was very unhappy. He complained about the situation. Clearly these new people were not well trained. After many years working with the same bank, Mr. A was planning on changing banks. This author believes that the cost of no training is greater than the cost of training. But when the employee turnover is high, training becomes a costly proposition.

The last item in the direct cost categories in Exhibit 10.1 is the cost of developing a worker in time to perform well. Again, when the employee turnover is high, these efforts become simply too costly.

Perhaps the most critical problem for a small-scale independent which is trying to personalize its customers is having unhappy workers who are treating the customers badly. There is no way of measuring the cost of such a problem accurately, but it could be devastating.

Add to mistreating costumers, unhappy workers do likely not want to come to work and are not motivated to do the job right. They may call in many times claiming that they are sick. Not only are they not willing to do the job well but they would try to not to do the work and not to come to work as much as they can.

Finally, unhappy workers not only spend much time looking for another job, but some of them may also share trade secrets, if any, with prospective employers. This, again, could be a very costly proposition.

Our discussion thus far strongly suggests that giving good working conditions to employees and treating them well is extremely important. It may not be quite conventional but treating its employees well as an asset and not a liability; in short, giving them a good job and investing in them is not only "good policy" but for smaller independents is a major strategy.

Good Job Strategy

As it is known, Walmart is famous for being a discounter, but also infamous in its efforts to keep the labor costs as low as possible. Store managers are strictly instructed to reduce labor costs. They resort to not being unkind but at times make questionable practices of paying less than what their workers rightfully earned (Ton 2014). Their standard defense is that we "must keep our costs low." This situation may not hurt Walmart necessarily, but Ton (2014) maintains that the smartest companies invest in their employees. This, in the long run, lowers their costs and improves their performance. In other words, giving good jobs to workers is a wise move. This author believes that it is simply a necessity for small-scale independents.

Good Jobs Strategy

Why is it that low-cost retail jobs are well known for low pay and minimum benefits, yet are unstable at scheduling and unreliable for continuity? The question is why provide such poor jobs and conditions to almost 20 percent of the labor force who are employed in the country.

Just why is the dogma of keeping labor costs to a minimum guiding the retail practice? Instead, provide good jobs and dignity to retail employees. In fact, it is maintained here that it is major strategy for smaller independents.

INVESTING IN PEOPLE PAYS

Companies such as Costco, Quick Trip, and Trader Joe's have been proving and enjoying the fact that investing in people pays (Ton 2014). Exhibit 10.2 presents a summary to indicate how providing good jobs to employees pays for the retailer. Although there are no clear-cut formulas or rules, the exhibit emphasizes three key points that will describe good retailing jobs. These are good pay, good benefits, and growth opportunities.

Exhibit 10.2 Investing in People Pay

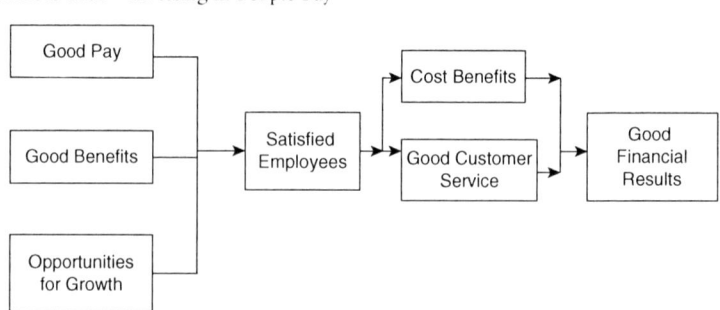

Good Pay

It is difficult to define good pay but one thing is clear, it is not minimum pay. The retail employee must receive reasonable income so that the whole concentration will be on doing a better job for the store. Obviously a good pay policy would include raises and fairness to make ends meet.

Good Benefits

Unlike prevailing poor treatment of retail employees, it is more beneficial to give them good benefits. These would include reasonable sick leaves, vacations, flex times as needed, and the like.

Growth Opportunities

The retail worker should not consider the current job as a dead-end street. Some retailers have promoted their employees, in time, to being department manager, buyer, and the like. The retailer must help the employee to get more experience, more education, and if possible a degree.

As can be seen in Exhibit 10.2, investing in people creates satisfied employees. This further creates cost benefits for the retailer and most importantly good customer service. At this point retail employees become a strategic asset. As they perform better, they create profit and success for their store.

MANAGING GOOD JOBS

Exhibit 10.3 introduces a general model of managing human resources which, by definition, includes good job management to be practiced. The exhibit begins with detailed job descriptions. Every retailer must know how many people are needed to run the store and what are the detailed description of the jobs to be performed. It will be an exercise in futility to hire people without having a good idea what they will be doing.

Employee Relations

All of the functions listed in the human resource mix presented in Exhibit 8.2 must be performed well. Retail employees are and should be engaged in personal selling and sales promotion, customer services,

Exhibit 10.3　Managing Human Resources in Retailing

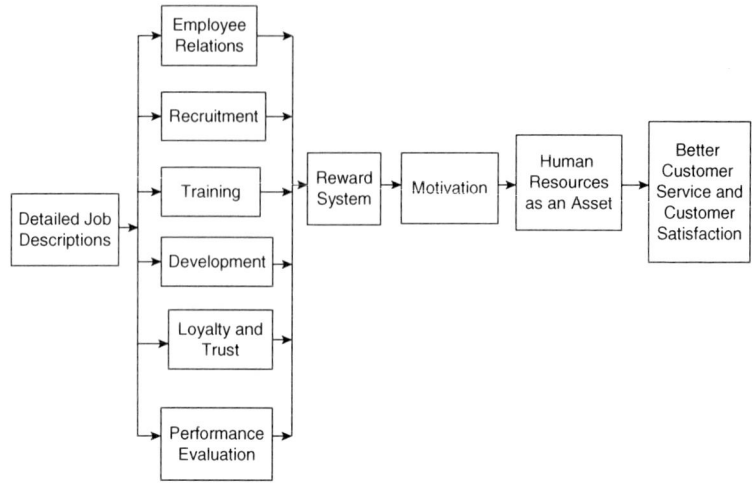

Source: Adapted and revised from Samli 2004.

and interaction with customers. Again this is one of the key advantages of smaller-scale independents which are connected to personalizing their customers. The employees must be constantly in touch with the store's management as to how these activities are being implemented.

Perhaps, in some cases, employees must have excellent merchandise and service knowledge. As a result, they should be able to advise customers on a large variety of merchandise selection and on care, repair, return, and the like. Retail employees are not only support people, but it is maintained here that they are a major part of the overall strategy particularly for smaller independents. In addition to keeping the establishment in good order, functional, and attractive, they perform regular duties such as delivery, assembly, and the like. But above all they personalize their customers and make the shopping experience a pleasant one. Certainly all of these activities reflect the story image and make it more attractive or unattractive. It is therefore clear that a highly competent and highly motivated group of employees must do their best so that the retail establishment can generate maximum customer value, which translates into profit. In order for the human resource mix to be a major strategic tool and create differential congruence, there must be a major human resource management activity in the retail establishment.

A HUMAN RESOURCE MANAGEMENT MODEL

Exhibit 10.3 presents a general orientation of a successful human resource management model (Samli and Ongan 1996). Employee relations are perhaps the essence of the whole process. Keeping in touch of all employees and working with them is likely to perform miracles. In many businesses when a person is hired, that person may get the feeling that he/she is left alone. The idea is to not challenge the worker; rather, it is to create the best shopping atmosphere for the store's customers by having happy and well-performing workers. In fact, they are not workers, they are associates.

Search Process

Locating, acquiring, training, motivating, and, above all, retaining qualified employees is essential for effective retailing performance.

As the retailer clearly identifies each position, its characteristics, what is expected from each person, it becomes clearer what type of a person is needed for those jobs. Here, the retailer must seek out the skills and talent that are needed. The specific sources of manpower supply must be specifically informed as to what types of persons are needed. These sources must be continuously evaluated in terms of the quality of employees they are supplying. Of course, this evaluation process revolves around how well the retail employees are performing.

Although sound recruiting is essential for the health and success of retail establishments, some retailers, particularly smaller ones, are handicapped in their ability to locate and attract quality personnel. Despite its might and far-reaching impact, since almost every 20th person is engaged in it, retailing has a long-standing negative reputation of not being an industry to get a job. It is known to pay very low salaries, not offering good, or any, benefits, and not providing opportunities for growth and advancement; furthermore, poor working conditions and questionable work hours are all part of this negative image. But the retail managers may not appreciate that their employees play a very significant role. This means for the particular retail managers not only try to get good, not necessarily cheap, people but seriously to sell their organizations' positive intentions to practice a good jobs strategy, which may help them to get the best possible people for their businesses. One more time, if the employees are not the right type of people for the job, they are not happy. They are not likely to go out of their way to make customers happy (Samli 2004; Ton 2014).

Many retailers, particularly smaller independents, think they lack resources to develop an effective human resource management system, must think twice. That is one key area that they can gain an edge over the discounters.

There is a bias on the part of retail managers that everyone must start at the bottom and work their way up. But this mentality does not encourage the best possible talent to seek a career in retailing. Additionally, part of their bias is related to the fact that employee turnover is so high that some managers feel as if they are training people for other retailers. Hence, they may not put their best effort forward in training newly hired personnel. All of these situations indicate the complexity of the retail human management.

Training

The retailing sector, in general, does not do a good job of training employees. Expenditures set aside for training are the lowest of any sector in our economy in absolute as well as relative terms. In this day and age there are countless opportunities for retail employees to be trained; however, these opportunities are not well utilized. Particularly smaller independents must make sure that their employees are continually improving, and as a result, serving the store's customers better. Instead, smaller independents generally consider training and putting more money into human resources not necessary, and therefore, they cannot develop core competency areas of personalizing their customers and create stronger, differential congruence.

But, perhaps the most important problem in retail human resource management is that they are not well understood that inadequate search and training do lead to employee ineffectiveness and turnover. It must be understood that worker inadequacy which is related to employee unhappiness and employee turnover is more costly than better screening and training programs. After all, constantly finding new people and providing them with even minimal training are costly propositions. In well-managed retail establishments every employee knows how to perform the assigned task properly within a given period of time (Ton 2014). It must be understood that while Walmart is having over 70 percent employee turnover, Costco is having less than 5 percent. The cost to Walmart in that case is almost impossible to calculate and clearly, it may not enter into its profit calculations (Berman 2014).

It is ironic that whereas the human resource mix is so critical for the retailer's differential advantage, human resource management systems are not well developed and, in the case of smaller independents, may not even exist (Samli 2004).

Development

If a retail employee sees the job as a dead-end street and considers it to be temporary, there will not be any continuity. In other words, that employee, in time, is not likely to be formed into a good, flexible, knowledgeable, and fully productive retail associate. Proper selection and training are necessary, but not sufficient ingredients of this process. It is not necessary for the retailer to develop a type of atmosphere within which its employees can grow professionally and consider their jobs a career. There may be formal and informal in-house activities to provide the employees with additional required skills as the nature of the industry changes. With the proliferation of technologically complex products with advanced systems and procedures, as touched upon in chapter 8, which need to be learned and operationalized, employees play a more important role. In fact, in some cases, the qualified retail markets are so important that for every critical position there may be an understudy, even if this means having somewhat more than a necessary number of employees. It must be considered that customers complain not about having too many employees but too few (Ton 2014). The retailer, therefore, should be more careful and permissive in this area.

Loyalty and Trust

Motivated and well-trained retail workers can and do generate differential advantage because they are loyal and dedicated to the retail establishment. They are active in recommending products and providing information to their customers. If they are well trained, they can find lots of useful functions to do: such as checking inventory, ordering more stock, and organizing their sections of the store. They also can spend more time with customers and help personalize them so that customers will feel special and helped (Ton 2014). "Can I help you find anything?" is almost a lost statement in most modern retailing establishments which loyal and motivated employees are likely to utilize. It may be maintained that a prerequisite to employee loyalty is the presence of mutual trust. The latter cannot be accomplished unless an aura of fairness, understanding, and honesty is present. These are the conditions that Walmart employees question and therefore create over 70 percent employee turnover (Berman 2014).

An aura of job satisfaction can not only lower the cost of human resource management, but also make it more effective for both the retailer as well as the customers. A corporate culture that would encourage retail employees to feel they are part of the total picture and use their discretion in certain decision-making situations is very desirable.

PUTTING A SYSTEM TOGETHER

A functional well-performing human resource management system must be based on at least three elements: employee relations, performance evaluation, and reward systems (Exhibit 10.3). These three elements, if handled properly and fairly, would create one of the key strategic powers that may be the answer for the success of smaller independents.

Employee Relations

A combination of policies, guidelines, procedures, and, above all, good will by the retailer that describes its responsibilities toward its employees' responsibilities must be developed. Successful retailers have managed to connect their integrated benefit packages directly to the performance of their employees. These benefit packages are composed of intangible benefits such as recognition, as well as tangible benefits such as financial rewards. Unfortunately, there are no routine procedures developed that would be most beneficial and acceptable by both parties. Europe and Japan are rather ahead of the United States in developing such packages. Such packages, among others, must deal with career paving, career enhancements, skill enhancement, flextime, and team building by unions (Samli 2004). These are important issues in employee relations and over 17 percent of the labor force which is employed by the retailing sector should not be deprived of opportunities and growth that might be possible. Thus, solid employee relation systems including all of these, and possibly more, issues are likely to improve the retailers overall performance. Human resource management is a major asset and must be treated as such.

Performance Evaluation

Fewer than half of the retailers in the United States are estimated to have a systematic approach in evaluating employees (Samli 2004). Without a performance evaluation system, employees do not know what is expected of them; furthermore, it is difficult to inform them as to management's perception of their performance, and the employee's perception of how they are evaluated is blurred. Clearly stated job descriptions combined with carefully stated reward systems are typically lacking and are very necessary for the retail establishments to perform well.

Reward System

In general, the reward system in the retailing sector is simply not what it should be. Discounters such as Walmart are paying minimum wages to their employees and certainly are not rewarding the best performers. The lack of an attractive reward system makes it difficult to stimulate a good feeling of belonging and ambition to perform well on the part of retail employees and stimulate an overall high turnover rate which is costly for the society as well as the retailing sector. A clearly stated fair reward system would generate a positive behavior modification by using positive reinforcement. Instead, human resources are exploited by the retailing giants with a few exceptions. The employees are not rewarded for good performance, but admonished for bad performance. If employee pay is manipulated by the management to get more work from workers, which is being practiced currently by some discounters; this does not provide any latitude and must be given to the employees to satisfy customers; this somehow is not in the equation. In other words, enfranchisement (Schlesinger and Heskett 1991) which depicts the connection between workers and customers is almost completely ignored. Again, this is a critical area where smaller independents can gain an edge over the discounting giants. This, of course, would entail giving more freedom and responsibility to retail employees that may improve the retail establishment's sales and earnings, while less direct supervision is practiced by the management. This certainly would increase employee earnings, their job satisfaction, and then being more committed to the retail establishment where they work.

MOTIVATION

All of our discussion in this chapter leads in the direction of motivation. Directly or indirectly, it is implied here that a good job strategy is the key to better performance (Ton 2014). Without properly motivated workers, the human resource mix is not likely to create the needed differential advantage. Individuals working in retailing must be motivated to work both harder and smarter. This means better service for the consumer and greater consumer value generation. The reward system in retailing is the key motivator. Unless the reward system is brought up to a desirable level, which would be consistent with other major economic sectors, the retailing sector may not perform up to its potential. Reiteration the key message in this chapter, the reward system and performance must have a strong, positive relationship. Thus, motivation will lead to the presence of a highly functional and successful retail work force.

CONNECTING PEOPLE AND SERVICES

Every retailer must ask this question: "Are our customers satisfied with our performance?" And not the question of: "How can we cut down the labor costs so that we can make more money as soon as possible?" Performance leading to customer satisfaction refers to service as well as creating a satisfactory retail atmosphere. Our people in retailing must exhibit reliability, responsiveness, assurance, and empathy.

In this context, reliability implies providing services that we claim we provide. Responsiveness means keeping our customers informed about our ability to provide the services they need. Assurance implies courteous employees making customers feel safe and confident about their transactions. Finally, empathy stands for giving our customers the attention that they expect and deserve. Our employees must understand our customer' needs (Berman and Evans 2012). In small and medium-sized retail establishments in particular, there may not be a more critical factor to differentiate the store from its competitors than service delivered by the employees of the store (Samli 2004).

MANAGING QUALITY IN RETAILING

Retailers must build and manage successful teams. Building successful teams, by definition, includes good hiring, good training, good supervision, and developing a reward system leading to motivation. Without proper motivation, retail success is likely to be less than satisfactory. However, still much of the prevailing retail practices favor a "Theory X" orientation. Such an orientation includes strict supervision, narrow spans of control, reluctance to delegate, and generally exercising an adversarial relationship with employees. The modern retailer needs to at least experiment with good jobs programs that will create job enrichment, flextime, strong incentive programs, a positive payment program, and other unconventional activities. Such programs will foster active employee participation in the long run and more flexibility in decision-making and enhanced individualism for workers and more satisfactory personalization of customers.

SUMMARY

Developing a powerful human resource mix in particularly smaller independent retailing is critical, since this mix is a critical strategic tool. In this chapter a case is made for the development of a good jobs strategy. This is an advantage since retailing giants do not have a very good reputation for taking care of its employees and hence suffering from a poor image of unsatisfactory working conditions, pay, employee turnover, and service.

The smaller independents must understand the importance of searching and hiring the right people, giving them good training, and treating them as not lowly workers but important associates. Thus, generating enthusiasm, loyalty, and an atmosphere of mutual trust will help the modern retail managers to succeed. All of these efforts lead to a three-point human resource management program concentrating on employee relations, performance evaluation, and reward system. This three-point program will provide the basis for proper motivation, which is extremely critical for human resource mix to be a powerful competitive tool.

11

WE MUST COMMUNICATE WITH OUR MARKET

In our market system for a business establishment, retailing is not exception; not to be known by the prospective customers is perhaps the worst thing that happens. In the market system no business can afford to be a well-kept secret. The attitude that "well, they know we are here, and they will come" does not work. Many smaller businesses have the attitude that all we need is word of mouth; we don't need any advertising. This orientation is deadly wrong. As we know just because we are here does not mean success. Any business, particularly, a retailing establishment, must communicate with the market and in time attempt to project and maintain a store image.

With the name, reputation, and image, retail giants do not need anything more in terms of advertising but consider, for instance, a small local gym. Nobody knows it exists. It has, say, a nice sign, but if it is adequately located only the vehicular and pedestrian traffic know that it exists. Furthermore, it may be located inside of a mall here; only the people frequenting the mall may know that it exists. Certainly, somehow, it has to make sure that its existence is known by the community and even neighboring communities. But, that is not enough; it has to undertake proactive promotional events, such as special family week, member appreciation, special program for yoga, a series, say, on women's self-defense, special young people programs, and many, many more activities. The worse thing is inactivity. This author has been witness to a series of failures of gyms just because they simply did not initiate activity to create membership.

Consider, for example, a locally managed Hilton hotel. A nice place with a good location it serves the people trickling in. Well! One might question is that enough? The hotel can be engaged in multiple activities to create a local image and increase its business from border-line sustainable to a lucrative undertaking. In this case, for instance, having, say, a local fashion show, or an Irish evening in its restaurant, or sponsoring a small-scale but selective golf tournament, and a husband and wife tennis championship are examples. The alternatives are almost endless, but the hotel, at this writing, is simply not doing anything except serving its trickle down guests.

A deliberate and carefully calculated communication plan certainly takes speculations and questionable gossip out of circulation and replaces them with the type of information and bits of fact that help construct an image in the minds of prospective customers and activate the target market to frequent the retail establishment.

What needs to be understood is that the simple promotional activity possibilities in above two cases are simply a few of hundreds of possibilities. But the real key here is that these promotional activities do not necessarily yield revenue. It is not that they are taking place; the key is that they are taking place and promoted. Such promotional activities being advertised create the image of say being dynamic, being up to date, being traditional, and the like. It is the information about the activity than the activity itself that really counts. The smaller independent newcomer cannot afford to just stand there and hope to be discovered. The development and manipulation of the newcomer's and all existing establishments' store image cannot be achieved without promotional communication.

IMPORTANCE OF RETAIL COMMUNICATION

It must be reiterated that all retail establishments have an image, but the emergence and development of this image should not be left to luck. Proactivity in the communication process is a key ingredient in retailing success. A retailer cannot afford to wait and see how word-of-mouth communication among consumers is going to shape up. This author has seen many retail stores come into existence where the owner-managers would simply sit and hope customers would come in. This is a very dangerous process. Most of these establishments die before they reach maturity. A small gift shop emphasizing on imports from Latin America, for instance, was opened in a small, sophisticated university town where the tastes and incomes would make a good niche market for such a store. However, it had two big problems because of cost factors: the store was located in a relatively less-developed part of town and there was no budget for advertising. People did not see the store and they did not know that it was in existence. Those who learned about the store had formed wrong impressions. The end result was a dismal failure.

Image development begins with promotion. It is by using promotion that the store establishes its existence or the market's knowledge of its existence. Attempts to establish the desired image is accomplished through promotion (Exhibit 11.1). If and when a proper image is developed by promotional efforts, the store will be recognized and positive name recognition will take place. In a survey, it was found that less than 1 percent of the respondents knew the name and the nature of the Latin gift shop discussed above. Certainly without any promotion, the name recognition was dismal. As illustrated by Exhibit 11.1, if the store's name recognition is advanced, the attitude of its customers is likely to change for the better. The store's target market customers will be more attached to it. Positive attitude may also spill over into the submarket of those who might be more interested in the store if they knew more. Finally, enhanced name recognition may even spill over into the segments of the market that are not likely to be customers of the store, at least in the near future or as of now. All of these direct and indirect results of successful promotion of the store image bring about increased sales volume and more customer loyalty. Of course, if results do not show the expected degree of improvement in sales volume and customer loyalty, additional research may take place to further modify the image and its promotion. As can be seen in Exhibit 11.1 an adjustment mechanism or feedback must be considered so that the store's performance, as image being manipulated, can be measured, improved, or totally revised.

Exhibit 11.1   The Impact of Retail Communication

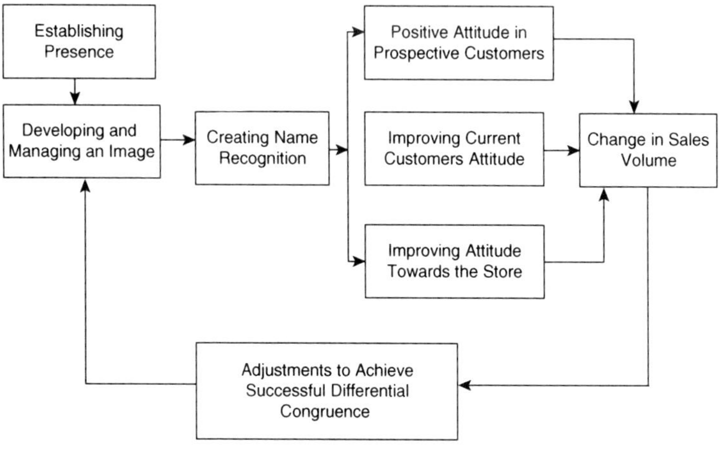

Source: Adapted and revised from Samli 2004.

Managing the Promotional Efforts

Although unplanned communication with the market revolves around and ends up being a part of store image, such efforts do not necessarily create the planned store image. Quite often efforts to communicate with the market have other, and perhaps more urgent, objectives such as promoting a special sale or publicizing a special activity. A gym may be advertising, say, for self-defense lessons for women, a local restaurant may be promoting a vegetarian evening, etc. Thus, it is necessary to distinguish the impact of certain promotional activity in terms of store image-building or institutional promotion and special activity promotion, which is sales-related promotion.

Consider, for example, an apparel store catering to middle-class consumers in a small college community. The store does reasonably well particularly with periodic special sales that are advertised in the local paper and displayed in store windows along with discount coupons sent out to regular customers. A research study authorized by the store indicated that the customers don't go there because of the atmosphere, ambiance, people, or the like. They go there primarily for the low prices the store charges and its special sales. Thus, there is not much store loyalty displayed by the customers. If the management of this retail establishment decides to eliminate the special sales and change the store's low-price strategy, the store can run into hard times. In fact, this is exactly what happened. The store was sold and the new management had a different overall strategy in mind the end result is that in six months or so the store failed. This author has seen many such situations. For this particular store if it were to attempt to develop better customer relations and promote these activities carefully, creating differential congruence of this type before the new management changed everything, it would have been possible that it may have survived. Exhibit 11.2 illustrates a general plan for retail promotion.

Identifying Promotion Objectives

In managing the store's promotional activity, the first step is identifying objectives to be achieved both in the short run and the long run. Of course if this is a new establishment, above all, establishing a presence would take the first and highest priority. Some of the key considerations are discussed in chapter 1; suffice it to say is that the prospective market must know that this particular retail establishment is here and is in existence. Over and beyond establishing a presence

Exhibit 11.2 A Plan for Retail Promotion

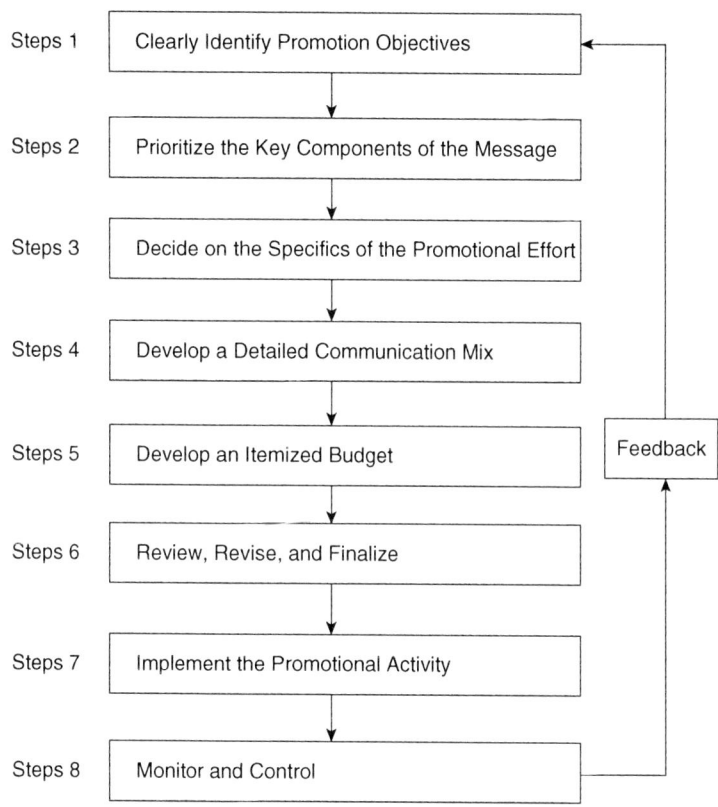

Steps 1	Clearly Identify Promotion Objectives
Steps 2	Prioritize the Key Components of the Message
Steps 3	Decide on the Specifics of the Promotional Effort
Steps 4	Develop a Detailed Communication Mix
Steps 5	Develop an Itemized Budget
Steps 6	Review, Revise, and Finalize
Steps 7	Implement the Promotional Activity
Steps 8	Monitor and Control

Feedback

in the marketplace, in regular considerations for promotional efforts it must be clear if the effort is related to promoting a special sales activity, meaning undertaking promotional advertising or the effort is designed to promote the store image which means institutional advertising. While the former deals with short run, the latter deals with the long run. It is maintained here that these two must be balanced. Although they may have some interactive characteristics, image-building promotion must be distinguished from sales and cash-generating promotions in the short run.

Prioritization of the Key Components

Even though short-run promotions are designed to create a reaction in the market toward buying a product or patronizing the store, it is important to think if the message is consistent or interfering with the store image that is also in the making. If the store is trying to establish an image of being a major art and art supplies establishment, it may not be participating in or sponsoring a starving artists show. Similarly, a female apparel store well known for its lower prices may not sponsor a higher-price fashion show in a well-known classy restaurant. There could be much similar examples. The objectives of the promotional efforts must be consistent with what the retail store is and where it would like to go. Sudden and dramatic changes in the promotional activity are not likely to make a contribution to the wellbeing of the retail establishment.

Decide on the Specifics of the Promotional Effort

Since there are more possibilities than what is needed, it is critical to prioritize the components of the promotional activity which is the communication mix. Consider, for example, a large international antique furniture and household accessory dealer who needs to advertise regularly and often. Visual impact of advertising for this retailer is critical, since imported collectibles change and new shipments arrive often. Furthermore, the target market must see how these products look, particularly in a particular setting. The question here is, just what would be the best, and affordable, media mix that will do the job.

Developing a Communication Mix

Once the objectives and specifics of the promotional activity are decided upon, it is necessary to decide how our messages are going to be delivered to the target market. It must be reiterated that unless we are a convenience store, our target markets are segments of the total population. Just what vehicles are likely to reach our target market is a critical question. If the message does not reach the target market and goes to other markets, then the whole effort becomes useless. A small independent retailer may use special vehicles to convey its message rather than a well-known retail giant. Smaller firms can use direct mail, flyers, social media, and the like. Certainly, in attempting to personalize customers, retail associates working in the store could be extremely valuable. Joint promotion with another retailer can be quite effective. Certainly the smaller independent may not consider using network television or expensive print media.

Developing a Budget

It must be noted that, unlike many retailers, establishing a budget upfront is not very functional. Once the nature, key points, and network needs are established, then it is time to add up the cost of all the planned activities and develop a budget figure. In other words, a buildup budget based on the estimated cost of all of the promotional activities, a "task objective" budget, is much more effective than what most people do. They set aside a budget figure, a total sum, and then they break it into components. This means dollars dictate the promotional activity top-down. This is not nearly as effective as bottom-up task objective approach.

Review, Revise, Finalize

This is step 6 in Exhibit 11.2. Once the cost of all of the promotional activities is added on, that orientation would generate a task-objective budget, but it is possible that the budget figure might be a little more than what we could afford. In such a situation it is necessary to review the whole promotional activity that is planned and perhaps take out the least important activities from the list which may bring the new budget to a manageable level. Thus, the promotional plan and its budget are finalized.

Implementing the Promotional Activity

The finalized promotional budget must also have approximate dates attached to it. Planning a promotional effort is quite different than the actual implementation of it. The implementation must follow the plan. If certain aspects of the implementation activity appear to be out of line, then it is critical to consider the whole promotional plan rather than simply making some adjustments willy-nilly.

Monitor and Control

The implementation plans of the overall promotional activity must be carefully followed, as well as monitored and controlled. Monitoring implies quick evaluations of, say, specific commercials, flyers, coupons, or other types of promotional activity. Control implies making some changes and adjustments as needed in these activities. The total outcome of the promotional activity can be evaluated by some attempts to receive a reaction from the consumers or from sales results. The results of the evaluation attempts would work as feedback for some key changes in the overall promotion program. Such feedback activity should become routinized so that the whole store performance can be improved.

ENHANCING THE SUCCESS OF
OUR COMMUNICATION

A retail establishment, any retail establishment, is constantly sending messages to consumers. Most of these messages are unplanned and uncontrolled—the way the store appears from the outside, the conditions of its restrooms, its layout, its atmosphere, and the like. Here a store is making claims by its promotional activity. The most damaging situation in this regard is when the store management believes that it is sending out certain deliberate or planned messages that are factual. But those messages are not perceived as factual. This kind of discrepancy is deadly for any store. There is a tremendous need for promotional consistency which means what the store claims through its promotions are accepted by the target market. What is being claimed and what is being perceived must be consistent if the store wants to survive. Here we advocate a "consistency theory" that maintains all messages both formal and informal that are coming out of the retail store, first, must be consistent. Second, they must be factual. But, third, and above all, they must be shared by the target market. Only with such consistency can the retailer establish credibility.

Exhibit 11.3 attempts to simplify this very complicated process. First of all management must identify all of the claims that are made through promotional efforts. Secondly, the management must try to identify informal claims that the store is not making but the store customers are perceiving. The second point is more difficult just how we identify informal claims that we are not making but our customers perceive. Here it is critical to go to research efforts and research techniques discussed in chapter 9. What our customers are thinking about our store is more important than what we think of our store and its outreach.

The third item in Exhibit 11.3 is very critical. Social media primarily deals with consumer-to-consumer communication. It is very critical to find out what consumers are thinking about our store. Much valuable information could be gained if social media evaluation can be obtained and analyzed. Smaller independents, it has been estimated, are not using social media as much as they should. All of the evaluations and claims need to be examined in order to determine

Exhibit 11.3 Enhancing Promotional Consistency

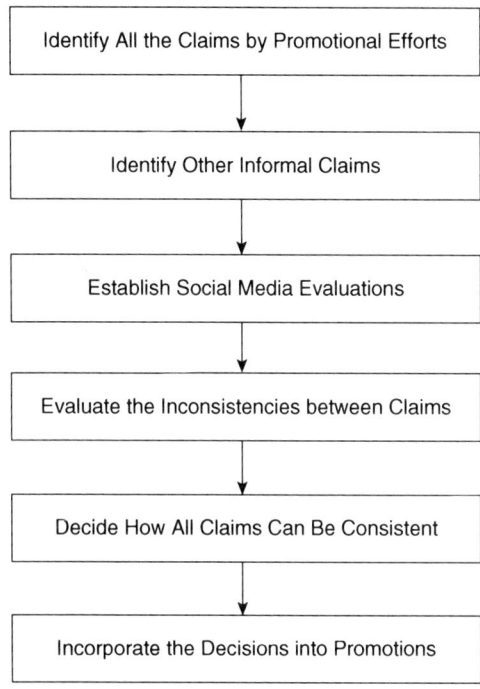

what, if any, inconsistencies exist among these. It is important to rectify this problem and make sure that all claims and all evaluations are consistent and positive. Here some critical decisions need to be made as to how such consistency in the promotional efforts can be achieved and how these decisions can be incorporated into the overall promotional efforts.

SPECIAL POINTS ABOUT SMALL RETAIL COMMUNICATIONS

Perhaps above all, it is extremely improper and dangerous to say "Well, we only have a small store and all this discussion presented here does not apply to our situation." With such an attitude, it would not be possible to survive the pressures of the retail jungle. Small retailers are even more in need of positive communications with their customers.

The lack of resources because of size may be remedied by creativity. Small retailers can be very creative in their efforts to communicate with their prospective markets and enhance their store image. Five such creative activities are articulated here—generating free ink, joint promotion, gift giving with purchases, general ambiance, and proper utilization of social media.

A retailer, particularly a small retailer, can benefit greatly by generating free ink. Free ink here is public relations. Having a story written in the local paper that did not cost anything is an extremely attractive proposition. The store may do something news worthy, for example, supporting local poor, or providing uniforms for the Boy or Girl scouts, offering certain collectables, innovating something that may be of public interest, or being the only gym in the area are all topics that could create free ink. All of these and many other developments could generate an attractive write-up in the local paper or be an interesting news item on local television. The value of such free ink can easily be greater than the total promotional budget of the store and it is almost totally without cost.

Joint Promotion

It is quite common for two retailers, or a retailer and a wholesaler or a retailer and a manufacturer to promote certain products and stores jointly. A local restaurant may have a fashion show by a neighboring apparel store. Similarly, a local jeweler may promote jointly with a local tourist activity. Many stores can give promotional discounts by giving discount coupons to their customers. Local museums can have a special evening sponsored by a local antique dealer. Similarly, an ice cream parlor located to a popular restaurant may offer the restaurant's customers, who do not want to eat heavy deserts, some pleasing frozen yogurt considerations.

Of course, cooperative advertising is also critical here. Some manufacturers and/or wholesalers jointly with the retailer may promote their products through cooperative advertising efforts.

Any time we can reach our target market customers through joint effort with others; it is worthwhile particularly if without that joint effort we cannot afford to create that advertising activity. Such joint promotion can work synergistically to generate additional business for us and for those who are participating in the cooperative efforts. There could be many other creative promotional activities that small retailers, in particular, can use. Anytime the retailer collaborates with others to sponsor, say, fund raisers for some charitable organizations or sponsor some worthwhile community activity; it is very valuable since it keeps the store's name before the public eye.

Gift with Purchase

Gift with purchase (GWP) is rather common in department stores, where a well-known manufacturer gives free gifts or free samples with a purchase of some specified product. In smaller retailing this would depend upon the store's orientation; however, it is not really a common practice. Giving a red rose on Valentine's Day or giving a special gift on the customer's birthday can create much good will that can be considered as the store's competitive advantage. Although the gifts may not be the store's key product category or may not even be a product the store is selling, the GWP process could enhance the recognition of the store itself and create good will toward it.

General Ambiance

This is a special promotion category, which is touched upon in chapter 8, particularly important for the independent smaller retail establishment. Unlike supercenters or warehouse clubs, smaller independents can sell genuine ambiance, warmth, friendship, and casual shopping comfort. Particularly ambiance here is of great importance. Not only the merchandise, displays, and layout but also features such as music, smell, and other features are considered to be particularly critical in these establishments. A number of studies have shown that proper selection of music and overall aroma excluding from the store, combined with smiling faces of helpful personnel, as discussed in chapter 10, are all extremely significant in generating consumer value.

Perhaps it is critical to reiterate that personalizing customers is closely related to ambiance and must be paid attention constantly. This is a philosophical position that smaller independents must consider and put it into action.

Proper Utilization of Social Media

Social media is a new and fast growing way of communicating with consumers. Marketers in general consider it almost essential for their businesses (Stetzner 2014). Over 92 percent of small business owners indicate that the social media marketing is effective at engaging current customers and attracting new ones (Derickson 2013). On the part of the consumers, one point is critical. A large number of them in a survey indicated that social media influenced their choice of retailer (Anonymous 2014).

These few bits of information indicate the need for social media usage. Particularly smaller independents must use this particular group of vehicles to reach out to their target markets.

Summary

Communicating with its market is not just important; it is totally essential for smaller independents to survive. Being a well-kept secret in the marketplace is almost deadly for a retailer. In the communication process the store's image must be promoted. Such promotions will enhance the name recognition of the retail establishment. It will stimulate a positive attitude in the marketplace toward the retailer. As a result, reinforce or improve the attitude of the target market toward, say, our store.

An eight-step promotion management plan is presented here. These eight steps are: identifying promotional objectives; prioritizing the key components of the message; deciding on the specific efforts of the promotional effort; developing a communication mix; developing an itemized budget; reviewing, revising, and finalizing; implementing the promotional activity; and finally monitoring and controlling.

It has been a distinction made between institutional promotions versus a cash flow-generating promotional activity. Both of them are important but typically must be kept separate.

Perhaps one of the most important messages of this chapter is that small retailers need promotion equally and perhaps even more than their gigantic counterparts. In making the promotional activity effective, the retailer must make sure that the formal and managed messages are consistent with informal and unmanaged messages. Without such consistency, the retail store cannot be successful in communicating with its market.

Finally, five special types of promotion are pointed out to be quite appropriate for smaller retailers. These include using free ink, engaging in joint promotion, practicing gift giving, developing proper ambiance, and perhaps most importantly using social media.

12

DEVELOPING A MERCHANDISE MIX

It is essential to realize that a retailer, any retailer, survives by providing its customers not what it wants but what the customers want. This may not be a problem for discounting giants since they offer everything but it is a big issue for smaller independents. They must offer important value to their customers that would make the quality of their lives better. For the retailer this means survival and perhaps prosperity. The retailer has to perform a number of functions related to product and service assortment. The process is called merchandising. There are four key components of merchandising: buying, planning, managing, and controlling. These four components must lead to, above all, providing the store's customers a highly desirable merchandise mix. This mix needs to be adjusted as the needs of the store's target market customer's change. In order to develop a desirable and adoptable merchandise mix, there must be a certain type of preplanning process, which is supported by an adjustment system. All of these activities are preceded by an effective buying plan.

DEVELOPING A VERY DESIRABLE MERCHANDISE MIX

The essence of retailing is to provide a desirable goods and services mix to a specific target market. The critical question here is just what are the characteristics of a very desirable merchandise or service mix. The answer will vary depending on the realities of each retail establishment. Some key generalizations to create a very desirable merchandise mix are as follows:

- The merchandise mix of our store has to be somewhat unique to our store, preferably different from our closest competitors.
- Needless to say, the merchandise mix must be very attractive to the customers in our target market.

Exhibit 12.1   Different Assortment Strategies

1. Deep and Narrow Assortment	Mostly a specialty store orientation
2. Deep and Wide Assortment	A general merchandise store approach
3. Shallow and Narrow Assortment	Typically utilized by convenience stores
4. Shallow and Wide Assortment	Mainly a discount store orientation
5. Consistent Assortment	A merchandise mix philosophy
6. Flexible Assortment	Whatever is discountable or whatever is available locally

Source: Adapted and revised from Samli 2004.

• Our merchandise mix must be most up to date in terms of recent incremental innovations performed by the manufacturer.

There are six major retail assortment patterns. It is critical that we must know which one is our most appropriate pattern. Exhibit 12.1 illustrates these six assortment strategies. If we want to be, for instance, a discount store, it will be necessary for us to have a wide assortment. Not being a giant discounter would mean having only a few units of each product. But it will not be wise for us to have a deep and narrow assortment where we have many units of a limited assortment and act like a specialty store.

Perhaps items five and six are particularly critical for small retailers. The question is, say, to have high quality of merchandise or simply what is discountable and what is locally available. These are two critical assortment orientations that the retailer must choose one of. The retailer must strictly follow one of these if the store is likely to have a reliable image.

Changing Consumer Needs and Adjusting Merchandise Mix

In dynamic markets consumer needs and consumer behavior change constantly. This is briefly presented in the Introduction of this book by referring to the retail jungle. But it is necessary to survive in this challenging atmosphere. Merchandise mix adjustment is one of the keys for survival and progress effort. Here it is critical to understand just what is happening to consumer needs. They are changing. Exhibit 12.2 illustrates some of these changes and what they mean to retailers. It is necessary to follow these changes and adjust the merchandise mix accordingly. Smaller independents must be in a position to detect new trends in consumer behavior and preferences. The earlier these trends

Exhibit 12.2 Changing Consumer Needs

Consumer Preferences	Retailing Implications
Personal appearance and self-consciousness	Need for more grooming and apparel lines, along with home exercise equipment and food supplements.
To become more casual	Retailers must carry more casual products in apparel lines, lounging furniture, etc.
Better health care	Retailers must carry more exercise-related apparel, equipment, and other products, along with health foods and health food supplements.
Leisure orientation	More emphasis must be put on leisure-related products, computers, computer games, videos, DVDs, entertainment centers, etc.
Some unique new luxury products	Satisfying consumers' special luxury treatment of themselves
Time consciousness	Retailers have to carry more efficient products, power tools, and more powerful computers and must put much emphasis on trading on the Web.
More home improvement	More retailers are providing home improvement supplies, along with advice for repair and decoration.
More pet orientation	Retailers must consider additional pet-related products and advice.

Source: Adapted and revised from Samli 2004.

are detected, the earlier the adjustments can be made. Certainly, this strategic stance depends on having good market intelligence detecting and reporting changes and an effective feedback system that enables the retailer to make adjustments very quickly.

Planning the Merchandise Mix

Since the merchandise mix is the retailers' life blood, it must be planned carefully. Such planning must get down to quantities, mixtures, and styles of the merchandise to be purchased by our prospective customers. Certainly these must be in reasonable quantities and carried in stocks for periods of time. All of these must be accomplished within the constraints of a budget that is manageable.

Earlier in dealing with differential congruence, it is mentioned that the merchandise mix is just about the most important strategic tool to create a powerful differential congruence. At least five key points need to be followed in developing a functional merchandise mix.

Merchandise Mix Planning

First, and above all, it is critical to make sure that, say, we know all the key product lines that are carried by our retail store. Without such knowledge it is not even possible to survive.

The second issue is to know how these key product lines are doing. Here it would be necessary to analyze the sales volumes of each category both in the long run, say, about five years and in the short run, about six months Although we appreciate long-term trends, we must place a little more emphasis on what is happening recently.

The third issue is clearly to identify the best and the worst product lines that are specified by the long- and short-run performance. Certainly it may mean placing more emphasis on the best and deciding if we want to even keep the worst product line.

Assuming that the retail establishment is closely connected to the developments of the local economy, the fourth issue is to identify the expected growth and development in the local economy. Local developments such as construction, population changes, infrastructure development, changing local competition, and the like would have significant impact on some retailers' merchandise planning. This is the fourth issue.

Finally, the fifth issue is emphasizing on the key product lines, adjusting it for local developments and trends. Here once again, concentrating primarily on the past six months or so may give us the basics of how the merchandise planning should be constructed.

This general orientation must modify further the basis of more specifics. If, for instance, the store has objectives to carry deep and narrow assortments (Exhibit 12.1) because it wants to be a unique specialty store, it will have to position itself accordingly. If, say, casual ware is one of the key areas the store emphasizes but it is offering too few varieties, colors, sizes, and styles, the retailer is not planning well. The other mixes of retail marketing strategy must also be adjusted. However, here our discussion is centered on the specifics of our merchandise mix. General merchandise plans typically are prepared for about six-month periods and reflect the retailer's perception of the relationships and associations among various products and other internal and external variables. In the preparation of general merchandise plans, two key areas are most influential. The first is category management (CM) and the second is merchandise control units.

Category Management

If the retail establishment is focusing on product categories rather than concentrating on specific brands or models, it would use the category management approach more readily. The approach arranges grouping of products into strategic business units (SBUs) and profit centers (PCs). Although this topic is briefly introduced in chapter 8, it is important to take another look at it from a merchandising perspective. Many retailers fail to fully understand the importance of this categorization and even differentiating SBUs and PCs.

In proper CM, the retailer would know which products or product groups that are offered in the store are more attractive to bring customers to the store. If these SBUs are working well, then there are other product categories in the store that can generate more profits. These are PCs that are carefully displayed and impressive choices for the customers to consider. Particularly in some larger retail establishments, the categorization of the products is done by some key suppliers who emerge as "category captains" (CCs). Their categorization may be somewhat different in each store of a chain. These CCs may play a significant role in managing the whole category (Desrochers, Gundlach, and Foer 2003). Although such arrangements can be significantly cost-saving activities, they may not be quite sensitive to the conditions that each unit may be facing. As a result, they are not effective in distinguishing and using properly the store's SBUs and PCs. Particularly in smaller independents, the CCs may not be effective at all. This is partially because there is not enough sales volume for CCs to pay adequate attention.

The fundamental database for CM needs to be drawn from a careful analysis of trading area needs. It is an important strategy of differentiation for the retail establishment in that it revolves around decisions of what to sell and what not to sell to a store's customers in its target market.

Even a very small retail establishment is like a combination of a number of businesses in that it has various merchandise groupings. It must be understood that all of these groups do not yield the same level of profit. It would be a big mistake to eliminate some of these products because they may not be yielding a desirable profit. The corner drug store in a small southeast university town had a very active lunch counter. One day, the lunch counter was closed forever. When this author inquired as to the reasons behind this action, he was told that the lunch counter was not yielding enough profit. This author asked the store manager if he knew how much purchasing the lunch crowd had been doing before or after eating lunch. The manager did not know. It is quite reasonable to assume that the lunch counter in this case was a SBU that brought the customers into the drug store so that the store could make money by selling some other products that are offered in the store which could be PCs. Some of the products may attract customers in the store that are the outreach of the store, and others would yield profit. The interaction between SBUs and PCs is the critical point in the CM. Here it is critical to realize that the retailer may be able to choose good product categories for SBUs and good product categories for PCs which is the ideal situation, and inability to choose poor categories of SBUs and PCs would be disastrous (see chapter 8).

Perhaps one possible but not common situation is having the same category for SBUs and PCs. In a general merchandise store, there may be a very good sporting goods section that is managed based on the characteristics of the target market which is a warm beach area with many other sports like tennis. The target market consists of a large group of younger people; the sporting good category may do very well as both SBU and PC.

Merchandise Control Units

In a more designated manner, the retail store must identify merchandise categories for which data are gathered and predictions are made. The gathered data identify narrow classifications of products that are called control units.

Control units are typically based on department-wide classifications such as jewelry or sporting units. In addition to department-wide classification, within a department classifications are also used. For instance in a jewelry department, certain lines such as fashion jewelry, gold jewelry, diamonds, and other precious or semiprecious stones can be featured.

The utilization of control units leads to three lists that retailers must have: basic stock lists, model stock lists, and never out lists. By using these three lists, retailers receive critical guidance as to managing the merchandise mix adequately.

Basic stock lists are detailed guidelines for key merchandise of the store with stable sales patterns. Since these patterns are predictable and their sales volumes do not vacillate significantly, basic stock lists can be very specific and carefully detailed. They can be utilized for planning future sales.

Model stock lists (or stock plans) are more readily constructed for certain shopping goods and fashion merchandise. They indicate, in some way, what should be available in a store such as this. The sales of these product lines fluctuate readily. They represent only a skeleton of certain sizes, prices, and quality and color combinations. These lists are not specific and detailed as basic stock lists.

Finally, almost every retailer has certain products that it is known for. The store should not be, indeed cannot be, out of these products. If a restaurant, for instance, is well known for, say, sweet potato fries its customers expect it to have them all the time. If the restaurant is out of them, once in a while, it creates a credibility gap among its customers which is not good for its business. The retail store is basically identified by its never out lists. They play a critical role on the store's overall image (Samli 2004).

All three of these lists are critical in selecting control units. In small retail establishments, standard merchandise classifications may be used as control units. However, every retail establishment has its own merchandise classification as well. Commonly accepted merchandise classifications combined with the store's own classification are likely to yield better results. Commonly accepted merchandise classification provides various computerized information systems. Data collected this way can be modified by the store's own classification and used for merchandise mix planning. Merchandise mix plans help establish stock keeping units (SKUs), which indicates groups of merchandise arranged for inventory maintenance and control.

Control Unit Utilization

Six specific steps are identified in developing control units—identifying control units, developing sales forecasts, planning inventories accordingly, allowing flexibility for reductions, making purchasing plans, and deciding on profit margins.

Since we have discussed the control unit identification process, here we begin with forecasting.

Developing sales forecasts. Although there are a number of forecasting techniques, here we prescribe a simple general orientation. The retailer must generate three sets of information. First, changing external factors, such as personal income in the trading area or changing population in that area, must be considered. Second, internal factors, such as total sales dollars or sales units and variations in these, must be examined. Finally, the seasonality factor must be taken into account since it is particularly critical in apparel, gift items, jewelry, and similar lines. When these three variables are combined, the following formula emerges: $S = F(X, Y, Z)$, where S = sales volume, X = external factors, Y = internal factors, and Z = seasonal factors.

If the relative role of each of these factors on store sales can be determined, then reasonable forecasts can be developed. Clearly, each store may have different experiences with these variables. Thus, the retailer must analyze its own sales and determine how these sales interact with these variables so that the sales volume can be forecast.

Inventory level planning is an essential component of merchandise mix planning. The retail store cannot tie up its limited and necessary resources in an inventory that is not moving in a necessary direction and level. If the store is overstocked, this can take away a large portion of its profits. It is critical that the store has adequate stocks so that it will neither lose sales nor be overstocked. It is essential that every retailer develops a system to plan timely purchases in adequate quantities.

It is extremely difficult to establish competitive advantage and survive in the retail jungle. With the new advances in information technology, large retailers have developed sophisticated merchandise mix planning systems. A major technique developed primarily for larger retailers is collaborative planning, forecasting, and replenishment (CPFR). This technique provides a holistic approach to total supply chain management. The system can deliver increased sales, organizational streamlining, and administrative and operational efficiency. As a result, cash flow improvement and return on assets advancement can materialize (Executive Summary 1999; Levy and Weitz 2012).

In order to process and fulfill orders in inventory management, quick response (QR) inventory planning, and electronic data interchange (EDI) are used by large retailers quite successfully. QR enables the retailer to reduce the amount of inventory by ordering more often and in smaller quantities. EDI, on the other hand, enables the retailer to use QR inventory planning more efficiently by enhancing the computer-to-computer relationship between retailers and their vendors (Levy and Weitz 2012). A retailer can use EDI to implement comprehensive strategies. EDI is a very sophisticated information network. It eliminates paperwork and facilitates information flow. It leads in the direction of creating more efficient ordering and receiving processes. EDI and bar coding combined have given retailers powerful tools regarding information base. These tools have been facilitating supplier-managed replenishment and automated ordering. Some version of data warehousing software dealing with managing different customer segments is also quite valuable here.

EDI and bar coding are facilitating CM and supplier-supported merchandising particularly in large retail establishments. They are not quite satisfactorily used by small retailers. Because of these sophisticated tools, large retailers are getting further and further ahead of small retailers. Small retailers need to find their ways to use the constantly emerging information technology so that they will not be too far behind (Samli 2004).

Planning the inventory is mainly based on three concepts: average monthly stock, average monthly sales, and planned monthly sales. The following formula may clarify how planned inventories are constructed:

$$PI = PMS + BS$$
$$BS = AMS_1 - AMS_2 \text{ therefore}$$
$$PI = PMS + (AMS_1 - AMS_2)$$

where PI = planned inventories, PMS = planned monthly sales, BS = basic stock, AMS_1 = average monthly stock, and AMS_2 = average monthly sales (Samli 2004).

It is essential that all retailers must be able to develop effective inventory plans. This is partially dependent on their ability to develop reasonable forecasts of monthly sales.

Planning Reductions

Markdowns are an important decision area in retailing. They may be used to stimulate the sales activity and in image modification. But even more importantly, they may be used to move some of the products in the store that are not moving fast enough. Although markdowns are primarily a pricing activity, they may have a critical role in merchandising activity. Reductions in general can also be part of the financial activity if, for instance, the store may need some quick cash. Markdowns may create quick sales and generate quick cash. For accounting purposes, some retailers may use shoplifting, which is almost inevitable in retailing, as part of the reduction calculations.

Planning Purchases

One of the key issues of being a smaller independent is that the retailer makes its own plans for purchases as opposed to chains stores. This could be a major strength if the retailer understands some of the unique needs and preferences of its target market. Having the inventory and merchandise mix planned at the head of a supply chain could be a cost-saving activity. But the planners of the supply chain cannot possibly know some of the uniqueness of each market. Nor are they sensitive to those unique characteristics displayed by each segment catered by the retail units of the chain. Thus, purchase planning could be an advantage of smaller independents over discounting giants. But it is necessary to understand what needs to be done, in order to capitalize this possible advantage. Planned purchases are calculated in the following manner:

PP = AMS1 + PMS+PMR

where PP = planned purchase, AMS1 = average monthly stock, and PMR = planned monthly reductions.

If there is a gap between planned purchases and actual ones in that much of the funds are not totally committed to routine purchase activities, the retail store has an open-to-buy (OTB) situation. This is a critical concept particularly in smaller retailing where some of the products are strictly coming from local vendors. This is a built-in flexibility situation to take advantage of expected and unexpected supplies coming from local vendors.

In order to take advantage of OTB situation, the retail manager must be familiar with the market segment that the store caters to but also must know local vendors well. A reasonable OTB situation under positive circumstances can provide real opportunities to take advantage of local unexpected occasions.

Clearly, purchase planning must establish how much is routinely needed to be reordered. Here a concept named economic order quantity (EOQ) is used. This is the quantity in a specific number of units that would minimize the total cost of processing orders and holding inventory at a certain level. Costs included in order processing are, among others, computer time, order forms, labor, and handling new products. On the other hand, holding inventory at a certain level includes costs such as warehousing, the cost of the merchandise in the inventory, insurance, taxes, depreciation, deterioration, and pilferage. Each store must be able to develop a reasonable EOQ of its own (Berman and Evans 2013). Such a formula can help optimize buying efforts by minimizing the costs of overstocking and losses from under stocking. The developments in modern information technology (IT) are facilitating such analyses to fine detail. Smaller retailers still have the problems of not using such techniques. Developing the necessary skills in these areas is a key to help cope with retail giants.

MERCHANDISE MIX NEEDS TO BE CONTROLLED

Thus far, our discussion relating to merchandise mix has been quantitative dealing with dollars and units. However, it is also necessary to discuss some serious qualitative aspects of merchandise mix planning. Two special areas are emphasized here: store image versus product image and the utilization of SBUs and PCs. Both of these areas provide important qualitative and managerial insights for merchandise mix control.

Store Image versus Product Image

Although the store's product mix may make a critical contribution to overall store image, products also have their own images. Most of these images are displayed by their brands. A highly recognized brand, say, Coca-Cola, may help improve the store's own image. Some small retailers try to develop their own private brands for their products. Although this could be important if it is successful, typically it takes time and cost to accomplish that.

Exhibit 12.3 illustrates the interaction between store image and unique products. Most small retailers may concentrate certain products that are unique and would attract customers. A local jeweler may be known for its diamonds. However, another local store may be carrying unusual gift items but may not have a specially known product line; it may not even be known for carrying gift items. As seen in Exhibit 12.3, the upper-left quadrant is very important. A sporting goods store in a resort area may carry collector item golf clubs. If the store has a good image to begin with, its unique product line can become rather synergistic. In the lower-left quadrant these special

Exhibit 12.3 Interaction between Store Image and Its Unique Products

Pull of Store's Unique Products

	High	Low
High	Ideal Conditions Store image and store's special products are reinforcing each other	Store Image itself is pulling customers. Store does not have unique products that are attractive.
Store Image Pull		
Low	Although the store does not have a strong image, some of its unique products are strong	This is the poorest situation. Store does not have a strong image, it does not have unique products either

product lines may be the only feature the store has. That is a rather weak situation. In the upper-right quadrant the store may not have (more than a few) very attractive lines, but overall it has a good image. Finally, the lower-right quadrant indicates not a successful situation. The store's future may be questionable if this situation continues.

SBUs and PCs Once Again

As partially discussed in this chapter and also discussed in chapter 8, identifying SBUs and PCs is rather critical. Many smaller independents may even be thinking along these lines. But it must be understood that every store must have an outreach and certain attractive products in the store. Balancing these two categories is essential in dealing with product mix management. Needless to say, having strong SBUs and PCs is the prescription for success in modern retailing. Smaller independents who are not well known, particularly, must plan their SBUs and PCs.

THE ROLE OF BRAND

As we discussed the need for unique products above, we also related to product brand image. It is necessary for smaller independents to utilize some well-known brands since it is difficult and costly to develop their own product brands. The manufacturer of the well-known products is interested in volume. Therefore, the manufacturer may not be too interested in offering a special deal to one single small retailer However, if the small retailer can team up with other similar and preferably not competing stores, it may be able to obtain a variation of a nationally known brand that is likely to help differentiate the retailer's store. Such competitive advantage can be very valuable. Furthermore, the smaller independent in time may attempt to develop its own brands, despite the cost and difficulties. If successful, that could be very valuable. The customers will know that they will find these brands and, say, designs only in that store.

As the retailing giants keep on merging and becoming fewer, large chains are becoming more predominant and the mass media sector is becoming more in demand but also more fractured because of the multitudinous mass media channels. Some store brands or private brands are gaining power. Proctor and Gamble, Unilever, Kraft, and many other similar national brands that are available on retail shelves are now facing competition from say, Kirkland Signature, which is found only in Costco stores (Boyle 2003). Smaller independents do not readily have this privilege.

BUYING THE MERCHANDISE

Large retailers have specialized buyers who do a critical job. Smaller independents do not have buyers. Managers generally cannot take time off to go to shows or visit suppliers and perform other functions that professional buyers perform. Smaller independents may collaborate with other comparable stores that are not competitors to do some joint buying. They may also use computers to do their buying.

Although there may be some automated buying, much of the time the owner-managers in smaller independents have to do this most essential function for survival themselves. Thus it becomes a necessary requirement for the store manager (or an assistant) to be well prepared to buy for the store. But the manager must be ready to undertake this critical activity. Exhibit 12.4 illustrates at least six skills that the store manager must possess in order to do successful buying.

If, for instance, the buyer for the store is very familiar with the target market of the store, good purchases would help the merchandise mix.

The buyer for the store must also know what merchandise lines are moving or not moving. The store's SBUs and PCs must be identified and adjusted accordingly.

A good sense of merchandise quality makes it possible to have the type of quality and the level of consumer value the store is known to generate. Treating customers as members of one's family is possible only in smaller independent entities. That is an important advantage that giants cannot achieve.

If the buyer for the store is not in touch with a variety of suppliers, then it will be difficult to get new merchandise lines or replenish the existing lines with better quality.

Perhaps one of the few advantages of smaller independents is flexibility. Having a reasonably open-to-buy policy enables the store to take advantage of some unexpected opportunities.

Exhibit 12.4 The Retailer's Readiness to Buy

Retailer's Skills	Conditions behind Practices
• Familiarity with the target market	Understanding consumers' needs and tastes
• Awareness of merchandise mix	Being familiar with merchandise availability
• Good sense of merchandise quality	Merchandise and quality knowledge
• Being in touch with suppliers	Knowing certain suppliers well
• Enough open-to-buy flexibility	Having a good control over the budget
• Good use of the internet	Keeping in touch with suppliers

Source: Adapted and revised from Samli (2004).

Finally, and perhaps more importantly, the retail buyer must be very interactive and comfortable with the Internet. Since the buyer is not likely to leave the store and go on shopping trips for the store, Internet communication with EDI and possibly some other lesser-known activities become extremely important to replace face-to-face communications that have been traditional in retail buying. These new techniques may facilitate international communications. International sourcing for small quantities of unusual products could be an advantage for smaller independents.

THE SERVICE COMPONENT

It is almost redundant to reiterate that smaller independents thrive on the service they provide. Personalization of their customers, if done successfully, is likely to give the smaller independents an edge. In fact, many smaller independents may not have any other strength besides offering good merchandise, comfortable and desirable shopping experiences.

SUMMARY

Without an adequate merchandise mix, retailers do not have much else to sell. The retailer will have to decide if the assortment is deep and narrow, deep and wide, shallow and narrow, shallow and wide, consistent or flexible. The retail assortment must reflect the changing customer needs.

In planning the merchandise mix, CM characteristics and merchandise control units must be identified. Merchandise control unit identification necessitates some type of forecasting, inventory level planning, reduction planning, and planning purchases. Since it is extremely critical for survival, merchandise mix must be controlled. This control activity dwells upon decisions regarding store image versus product image and distinguishing SBUs and PCs. A new era of utilization of electronic data and applying it to international sourcing needs to be considered by smaller independents. Buying for a retail store, particularly for smaller independents, is not only critical but it is totally a must. The retail managers must have some very critical skills to perform this very demanding function.

13

PRICING STRATEGIES

Obviously, without an adequate price policy the retailer cannot survive. Here the smaller independents cannot compete with the modern discounting giants, but it does not mean they cannot offer a reasonable price and provide a reasonable consumer value. Pricing is a complex issue. Many retailers shy away from doing research and experimenting with their own pricing strategies; as a result, many retailers place emphasis on the manufacturer's suggested prices. However, each retailer is different, and pricing should be, even in a small way, a part of this different identity. It must be reiterated, however, that while discounting giants are competing primarily on the basis of pricing, smaller independents can offer good service and make their customers not feel as if they are simply numbers.

A critical question is whether smaller independents can perform small and not very complex operations that may generate some pricing advantages. Even if this is possible, it should be only a plus factor. The smaller independents cannot win a price war.

But, on the other hand, one may ask a question such as: "would consumers prefer a large place with no personality but many discounted products piled up, or a store with extremely pleasant ambiance, good prices, excellent service where they feel they are important individuals"? The answer is that keeping our prices reasonable and competing on the basis of uniqueness and service certainly, at least some of the time, would be preferred.

PRICING OBJECTIVES

Any retailer can have one of a number of pricing objectives. If making money is the first and most common objective, the retailer must understand that in the marketplace, making money is the *reward* that is received from the customers, because the retailer with its services created consumer value. But the retailer may also be using pricing to increase the sales volume or to advance its market share, to create better return to investment, and to generate a short-run cash flow. None of these objectives can make an impact on creating target market satisfaction (Samli 2004).

If achieving a certain increase in the sales volume is taken as the pricing objective, then the retailer is assuming a high-price elasticity, which means if the price goes down there will be more than proportionate increase in sales volume creating a desirable increase in the total sales revenues.

If increasing market share is the pricing objective, then other considerations will have to enter the picture also. Among these are all other retail mixes (see chapter 2), the store's overall appeal, its success in creating differential advantage, and store's reputation.

Actual profit or expected profit creating an expected return on investment can also play an important role in a store's pricing activities. In the short run, for instance, to create cash flow, there may be a number of *loss leaders*. Similarly, some items may be priced higher to generate greater profit in the long run. This is a proper utilization of the strategic business units (SBUs) and profit centers (PCs) dichotomy which is discussed in chapters 8 and 12.

Smaller independents are much closer to their target markets than the discounting giants. Hence, the satisfaction of their customers must always be related to any and all activities they perform. If, for instance, some of their regular customers start complaining about certain prices, such indications must be taken into account immediately. If the target markets of the store are buying certain products offered by the store more than expected, that should not be an indication to raise the prices of these items. On the contrary, those products must be promoted even more. Identifying the target markets and serving them well is the key to survival for the smaller independents. The store and its customers both must be benefiting from their relationship. This is differential congruence at work and store's pricing decisions have a strong impact on this.

Clearly, gaining a larger share of the total market through pricing is certainly not one of the objectives of smaller independents. Discounting giants can be involved in a subtle or obvious price war that happens reasonably often. The smaller independents would not even think of such pricing practices since they cannot afford them. Discounting giants can survive a long time without making any profit in a price war. Smaller independents cannot possibly be in such a position. Amazon.com, a multibillion dollar retailer, did not make any money for years, but did survive. This orientation is totally out of question for smaller independents; they mostly do not have that kind of staying power in the marketplace.

PRICING GOALS

Exhibit 13.1 presents three major pricing goals, of these three the first two are perhaps more appropriate for smaller independents. However, the first one is more appropriate. The second one is somewhat applicable. The third one is not likely to be considered by smaller independents.

Passive Pricing

Passive pricing implies that the retail establishment is downplaying pricing as a strategic tool. It is basically putting concentration on other strategic alternatives and hence making the store management not to worry too much with the pricing, since they cannot compete with discounting giants. There are at least three separate practices dealing

Exhibit 13.1 Pricing Goals and Practices

Pricing Goal	Practices	Implications
Passive Pricing	Price lining	Grouping merchandise in to price categories
	Blind item pricing	Keeping a product unknown and unnoticed and pricing it slightly higher
	Copying competitors	Pricing the way competitors are pricing
Active Pricing	Direct profitability	Trying to maximize the profit contribution of each item
	Cost plus, a fixed margin for all products	Applying, for instance, 40 percent to all products
	Cost plus a variable margin	Pricing slow moving items with higher margin and fast-moving items with lower margins
Aggressive Pricing	Leader pricing	Market leadership aggressively lowering prices
	Skimming pricing	Charging high prices
	Pricing as a strategy	Being recognized as a low price store
	Knock-off pricing	Slightly different merchandise but much lower pricing

with this pricing goal. Price lining is a commonly used practice used to make shopping easier for consumers as well as for grouping merchandise to help management. Merchandise groups are usually specified with certain price ranges, such as low-priced group, moderate middle-class group, and a high-price group.

Blind item pricing is the second type of practice in this pricing goal. By keeping a product or product line reasonably unnoticed and pricing it slightly higher, a PC opportunity can be created. Obviously, the product or the product line has to be of interest to the target market when it is emphasized in the store.

The third passive pricing practice is simply copying competitors. This is simply making sure that the same product or the product lines are offered at the same price as the competitors offer. This type of me-tooism can be reasonably effective if the competitor is known for its consumer value generation.

Active Pricing

Here, the retailer utilizes pricing as a partially competitive weapon. But, it must be realized that, this retail store is not known for being a discounting giant. This retailer may see some possibility, however, to use pricing as one of its strengths. There are at least three types of practices in this pricing goal.

Trying to maximize the profit contribution of each and every item is rather proactive. However, as discussed particularly in chapters 8 and 12, all products or product groups may not be expected to yield profit. SBUs as stated earlier may attract the consumers to the store, where there may be certainly other products which we call PCs. Once again, the management's ability to first identify them to use product categories as SBUs and PCs is extremely critical. But profit contribution of SBUs is not the same as that of PCs. It is PCs contribution to profitability that needs to be considered.

A fixed cost plus pricing is the second practice category in this pricing goal orientation. This simply makes pricing rather easy and practical. Every product in the store is priced on the basis of cost plus an agreed-upon percentage such as, say, 40 percent. Cost plus a fixed margin is a common and popular approach used by many convenience stores. Why convenience stores? The key orientation is based on just what kind of inventory turnover the product is performing. In convenience stores typically most products have approximately the same level of sales and replacement rates. But in a store, say, an apparel store, some products move much faster in season and others move slowly. In such cases the cost plus a fixed margin may not be workable because of the varying nature of the products handled.

Here the third type of practice is cost plus a variable margin that is utilized. As discussed in chapter 3 some products move very fast. They are convenience products which consumers use them quite often. Such products are low priced to facilitate their replacement or reuse by consumers. These products must not be priced out of reach of the average consumer; typically, their pricing is based on cost plus a small markup. Similarly, some products are not purchased but once in a long while. They are typically higher-priced products and typically a cost plus larger markup is utilized to construct their price. Thus, variable margin becomes more reasonable if the store has both product categories: fast moving cheaper and slow-moving more expensive. This practice is difficult since many margins may be used for many products that the store offers. But this is a proactive practice indicating flexibility.

The third pricing goal has four different practices (Exhibit 13.1). Most of these are not appropriate for smaller independents. It is, therefore, critical that smaller independents must understand which practices are more appropriate.

Leader pricing means trying to establish a price leadership regarding a particular product or particular product line. In such cases, the retailer aggressively lowers prices to establish a certain identity of being a price leader in that trading area. It may be reiterated that the products with lower price, somehow, may still be SBUs but in these cases this situation is not quite obvious. In fact, all of the prices may be low and the store makes money by simply achieving large sales volumes as does Walmart.

Skimming pricing is just the opposite of the above practice. It implies charging high prices and selling just small quantities. This is rather typical for well-known luxury products retailers or very well known jewelers. In fact, they are expected to have high prices. A well-known local jeweler may use such pricing selectively for some of its key products. A store which has a reputation for selling unique and expensive products will not survive by using skimming prices unless everyone knows that one receives good value there.

Some retailers may use pricing as an overall strategy. Certainly Walmart does that. This is the third practice in exercising an aggressive pricing goal. Here establishing a reputation to be a low-price establishment and staying with it is the practice. Certainly, at times this pricing practice is a great advantage for customers. Smaller independents are not able to accomplish that. This is why they really rely on convenience, service, and treating customers one at a time. They need to be very careful making their prices as reasonable as they can, but not emphasizing it as their key strategy.

Finally, knock-off pricing implies a low-priced secondary line. This should not be used by those who thrive on reputation and valuable merchandise marketing. It may be used rather easily by second-hand stores and stores may concentrate on selling to the poor.

If pricing is not going to be the focal point which is the case for smaller independents, perhaps neutralizing the store prices may be a reasonable orientation.

NEUTRALIZING PRICING ACTIVITIES

Deemphasizing pricing by smaller independents is important. Their customers go there for convenience, good treatment, being paid attention to as individuals and good purchases, and the like. But in all of these cases price must be considered as a given by customers. In that, the retailer would not take advantage of you. This condition particularly requires certain pricing practices that are put forth in Exhibit 13.2. Although not an exhaustive list, the exhibit identifies five different practices that the smaller independent must consider just to neutralize pricing.

The smaller independent must, above all, be consistent. This means they do not vary their prices for different customers. The same product, say, with different colors would not have different prices. They provide good value at reasonable prices for their products.

The second item in Exhibit 13.2 is positive responding, arguing with customers, if they have a complaint regarding pricing, it is totally unacceptable. In the marketplace, bad news spreads much faster. If the store is labeled as unreasonable and unfriendly, it becomes impossible for it to survive.

Exhibit 13.2 Neutralizing Pricing

Practices to Consider	Application details
• Be consistent	Do not vary prices for different customers
• Respond positively	When a customer complaints about some aspect of pricing make the adjustment immediately
• Prices must remain the same	But this product was cheaper last week is a poor observation to hear from a regular customer
• Never laid and switch	Do not promote a product at a price that you do not have
• Greed does not pay	It is not how much can you get now, it is repeat sales that must be considered

Prices must remain the same. If the prices change, say, from one week to another, customers lose confidence in the store. This is an irreparable situation. It could create the concept of bait and switch practice. "Bait and switch" is rather commonly used, unfortunately, quite often by smaller independents. Advertising a product at a great price, but in reality not having it is not only illegal but is quite unethical. When the customer comes the store and asks for this product saying that it is sold out, but a more expensive alternative is available is a practice that, this author maintains, it is a reputation killer and good marketing in smaller independent stores has no place for such practices.

Finally, the smaller independent should not try to "make a killing" by one transaction or two. It is not making as much money as you can in one time but creating and maintaining continuity by repeat sales to loyal customers. This is the orientation that must prevail. Thus, greed does not work.

CONNECTING GOALS TO STRATEGIES

Category killers such as Toys "R" Us or Walmart, knowingly, or unknowingly use basic economic principles. When Walmart states "save more and live better," there is an assumption that consumers must concentrate on discounted pricing for better living. If the retail prices are lowered, classical economic analysis indicates that demand goes up and more units are sold. If more units are sold, then costs are being driven down further. This situation can help to reduce prices even further and, hence, helps the retailer to sell more. Such a cost-driven pricing strategy employs aggressive pricing and keeps prices below market. But this is not the whole thing. As discussed in different sections of this book, people do not engage in retail buying only for prices. This is where the smaller independents are and they must utilize other price conditions. It must be reiterated that a neighborhood convenience store does not compete with national retailing giants on the basis of price. Smaller independents exchange convenience and good treatment for lower prices. They can do very well with passive pricing goal practices. They need to use other retail mixes well.

SPECIAL SALES AS A STRATEGIC TOOL

Argibrites was a men's store in a university town that was owned and managed by four generation of Argibrites. The store has always done well, but twice a year it offered spectacular sales that were well known and extremely popular. The newest generation of Argibrite's manager decided to get rid of the special sales and use slightly higher prices throughout the year. The store closed down within a year. Once again, smaller independents must understand and use special sales very carefully. This author has known of presale parties by invitation only and has often heard special sales described in words such as "the sale this year will be better than ever before," repeated throughout the year. Even though 30 or 40 percent of the store's business may come from such events, genuine sales generate much value for the store's customers and are a constant promotional activity foundation for the store itself. Special sales can be used by any small retailer regardless of pricing goals and strategies. Planning and implementing these events are critical activities and must be taken very seriously.

Summary

It is clear that without proper pricing, particularly, the smaller independents cannot deliver the product or the service. Pricing, therefore, is a critical aspect of retail practice. If the retailer wants to survive the retail jungle, the store must have a good price mix. In this chapter, the key emphasis is placed on pricing goals. Three such goals are identified: passive pricing, active pricing, and aggressive pricing. Of these the first two are more suitable for smaller independents. The smaller independent must not use pricing as it is used by discounting giants. But, at the same time, they should not take advantage of their customers by some questionable pricing practices.

14

BEING CONNECTED TO
A SUPPLY CHAIN

M any small retailers are connected with a large retailing line either as being one of the stores in the chain or being in a franchising arrangement. This connection would modify independent decision making and further modify the flow of products which we call here logistics, despite its cost benefits being connected to a supply chain would limit freedom of the retail unit in many different ways.

Exhibit 14.1 presents some of the main advantages for not being a part of a supply chain where the decisions are made for you at the point where supply chain is generated. A good marketing manager making key decisions for the retail establishment is in a position to make some key adjustments as local conditions may require or as the local conditions change. For, say, a sporting goods retailer, if a big local tournament won, the retailer may be in a position to create a major advertising campaign based on this major event which would not be authorized or approved by the originator of the supply chain.

Similarly, local conditions may require a somewhat unique product mix, again, which would not be allowed by the supply chain.

It is possible that the retail establishment exits in an area where there may be numerous small manufacturers producing a variety of products which are quite appropriate for the smaller independent to market, then this becomes a strong position for the store. The decision-making unit for the supply chain would not even think of such a possibility. But an independent retailer with carefully planned open-to-buy provision can utilize this opportunity to buy some unusual but very attractive local products to be offered to its market segment.

In reality, the decision makers for a supply chain cannot possibly identify and manage each unit's strategic business units (SBUs) and profit centers (PCs). This is a very difficult task for a central authority since each unit in the supply chain deals with somewhat different market conditions. It is not possible, therefore, to have one standard SBU

Exhibit 14.1   Advantages of not Being a Part of a Chain

Advantage	Reason for Practices
• Being able to adjust activities to local conditions	Each market and each segment is different
• Using general product mix accordingly	There are no national or international fixed product mix
• Developing a varying promotional activity	The changes in the market segment of the store may necessitate changes in the advertising plans
• Ability to manage SBUs versus PCs	The store is in much better shape to decide on SBUs and PCs
• Out of store logistics adjusted to the store's needs	A logistics activity by a supply chain is more in favor of the chain
• Instore logistics adjusted to the store's needs	The planning unit of the supply chain cannot possibly do a good job in each store
• Being able to use local supply opportunities	The planning unit cannot possibly be aware of local product availabilities which are a big bargain

and standard PC categorization which would be applicable to all units in the chain. Each unit must act according to its unique conditions.

Every store is different in terms of economic conditions, location characteristics, and merchandise mixes. The logistics of merchandise flows from manufacturers are quite different for each store. Again, it may be impossible for a central authority to make decisions that would apply to all units in the chain. An independent unit may be able to make better decisions for itself.

When it comes to in-store logistics, that is, moving and arranging merchandise in the store, once again, different retailers present different personalities which, among others, is displayed by the store's decor and internal layout. Having a central authority that would create very similar looking units may be good for discounters or other gigantic chains, but it would be terrible for an independent trying to establish a differential congruence.

It will be an error, however, to deny the advantages of being part of a supply chain. All fast food chains have stores that are basically alike. In such cases, the cost advantages of developing and running a retail unit may be rather attractive. Furthermore, in such cases major decisions are made at the headquarters which makes it easier to run the individual units. But, as posited here, smaller independents making their own decisions under the varying condition is essential.

OUT-OF-STORE LOGISTICS

In chapter 8 logistics concept is briefly introduced. It is one of the five key retail mixes. In general, logistics involves the total process of successfully moving the merchandise from manufacturer or wholesaler to our store in a most timely, effective, and efficient manner.

This aspect of logistics deals primarily with order processing and fulfillment, transportation, and warehousing. Out-of-store logistics, particularly in large-scale retailing, has been spilling over into in-store logistics as well. By combining the two, suppliers maintain a total value delivery to consumers. In many retailing giant's operations, these two types of logistics are both treated almost automatically, but mostly in terms of cost efficiency. Suppliers or logisticians in this sense have been playing a critical role. However, the picture is quite different in small scale retailing.

Small retailers are not able to receive the cost benefits of out-of-store logistics. They also contact suppliers to share some of the merchandise outside the store, and take delivery, and do other similar out-of-store logistics functions which are all in much smaller quantities. Unless they can find suppliers dealing with smaller volumes, of course at a higher cost, or can team up with other retailers and buy jointly, they cannot receive the same benefits as discounting giants. Perhaps the smaller independents do something that may have out-of-store logistics strongly supporting in-store logistics in terms of generating customer value.

In contacting their suppliers, small retailers also can use electronic data interchange (EDI), bar code, and other information technology (IT) means of communication to accelerate the communication process almost as easily as large retailers. But, in this communication process, the small retailer is able to process its in-store logistics activity and carefully connect that to out-of-store logistics. If that can be achieved, then smaller independent may be able to accomplish a major task that would make its customers more able to shop the right merchandise in right settings. Large-scale retailers would not be engaged in such activity; it would not make any difference in their costs.

To the extent that small retailers can forecast their sales, partially based on their inventory requirements in a methodical manner, they can order electronically and meet the proper combination of volume requirements. Thus, they can connect in-store logistics with out-of-store logistics system tightly. Particularly some companies, such as GATX Logistics and Ryder, are making some effort to help small retailers. As competition among logistics firms increases, there will be more logistics companies trying to help smaller independents. This would be a great benefit to the national economy as a whole.

Out-of-store logistics costs, certainly, can be reduced if some small retailers can enter into a joint agreement with some other small retailers to buy jointly.

A large women's specialty retailer in Canada, for instance, has developed a distribution center. It ships millions of garments throughout 600 stores in Canada. It runs primarily on automated receiving, automated processing, and automated shipping. It has been working on its distribution accuracy, labor requirements, and processing time (Berman and Evans 2013). This is the type of out-of-store logistics that larger retailers can employ. But certainly a similar type of activity starting from bottom-up that can be organized by a number of smaller independents cannot accomplish that. It is still questionable if smaller independents do have the initiative, will power, and courage to organize such logistics systems.

Although smaller independents may not have the same advantages as the discounting giants, they have other advantages. As mentioned earlier, smaller independents working with reasonable open-to-buy accounts can adjust their out-of-store logistics costs by buying from local procedures. Additionally, they may buy more unusual merchandise that would appeal more readily to their target markets and help enhance more readily their target markets and help enhance their store image as well.

More on In-Store Logistics

In smaller independent retailing units in-store logistics may be and should be used more effectively than the discounting giants. As discussed in chapter 7 personalizing retailing activity and adjusting the store to customer needs, and creating shopping conditions accordingly are part of the in-store logistic considerations. Positive human resource mix combined with attractive store layout and very appropriate inventory all help differentiate the store. In-store logistics, here, play an important role in that effort.

Consider, for instance, the following:

A large retail establishment, dimly lit, with hard floors, merchandise piled up in groups and no one ever is available to ask for directions or to find what you may be looking for. You are not sure where you are and where you want to go.

Although some people may not mind these negative conditions since they are only thinking low prices, many others may prefer convenience, comfort, and relaxed atmosphere, where the layout is known to them and the people are friendly. In fact, they may know the people who work in the store well. Therein lies the critical role of in-store logistics.

Exhibit 14.2 points out the fact that in-store logistics may decide how and how much out-of-store logistics are going to be utilized.

Based on customers' purchase patterns and their particular expressions, the store's total sales and inventory control performance are enhanced. The store layout plans and makes sure that there will be, if any, minimal inadequate supplies in the store, the smaller independent is facilitating its in-store logistics. These in-store logistics-related activities would help determine merchandise mix. Once it is decided upon how this merchandise is distributed within the store, the smaller

Exhibit 14.2 Small Retailer Logistics

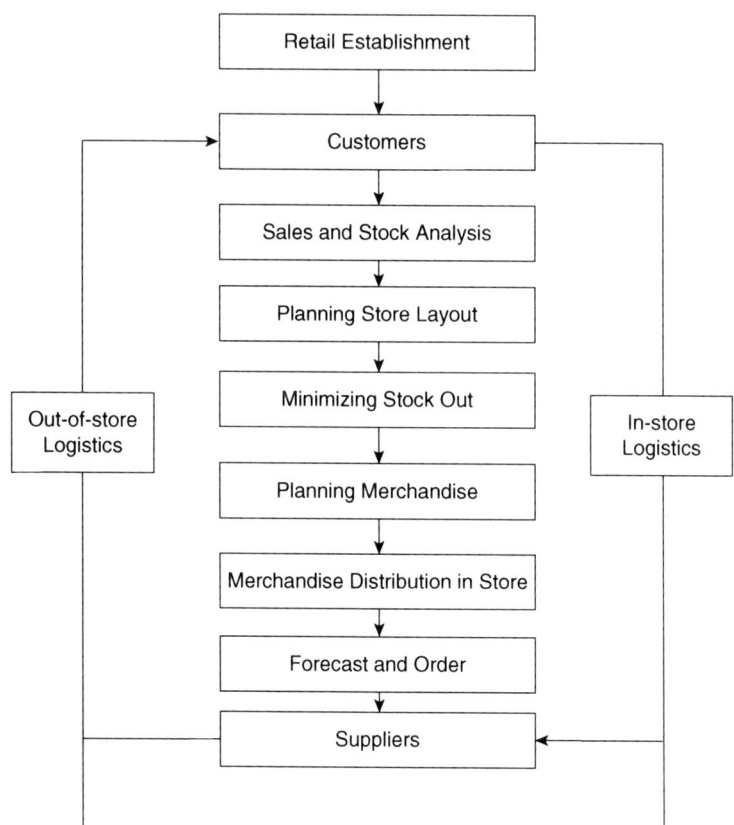

independent is ready to determine what, how much, and when. Using such forecasting information to order is very effective. The suppliers would respond to the retailer in terms of out-of-store logistics. This is a much tighter connection of in-store and out-of-store logistics activities. In order to get this tight connection, Exhibit 14.2 presents the key parameters of merchandise planning. This is the critical focus of in-store logistics (Progressive Grocer 1995; Samli 2004).

Merchandise Planning

Arranging merchandise categories, certainly, cannot be a haphazard activity. As can be seen in Exhibit 14.3, merchandise categories need to be arranged as if consumers are doing the arranging themselves. Products must be easy to find and naturally easy to examine and compare.

Although it is important to categorize products in the store on the basis of *time*, say prominently displaying new models or most recent fashions, on the basis of space. Also having fast-moving small items in one area as opposed to slow-moving big-ticket items in another area, and on the basis of *product situations*, such as displaying accessories next to most fashionable dresses, there must also be an *aesthetic* match. Arranging the products in a pleasing manner calls for creativity, vision, artistry, and as discussed in chapter 8 small data.

If the categories are carefully connected and complement one another, then, in addition to being aesthetically pleasing, they may lead to multiple purchases. Opportunities for multiple purchases are planned; there may be some emphasis on joint pricing along with

Exhibit 14.3   The Key Points of Merchandise Planning

- Arrange categories as customers would if they were in charge. In other words, make them easy to find, easy to evaluate, and easy to compare.
- Categories must not only be based on time, space, and product utilization, but also on how they match esthetically in terms of color, functional connection, and creating a pleasing appearance.
- Display must lead in the direction of multiple purchases by placing complimentary products close to each other.
- The aim is to create unique customer value evident in the personality of the store, whcih value in turn adds to that personality.
- The category management reflects the needs, values, and preferences of the store's trading area.
- The retailer must as clearly know what the store should not carry as what the store should carry.
- In managing categories, the emphasis is not only a single SKU but combining related SKUs in the form of an attractive category set.

---

aesthetic and functional matching of the merchandise. A certain evening dress may go particularly well with certain stylish accessories and, hence, such a situation may lead to multiple purchases, if they are located close to one another and if some discount system may be used in pricing these two groups.

Shopping in a store that is aesthetically soothing, it is maintained, psychologically can create consumer value. The personality of the store, if it matches the buyer's personality, creates strong differential congruence.

Merchandise planning encompasses multiple category-management activities. Certain product category groups need to be managed in such a way that combined they provide the perfect merchandise selection and display the trading area of the retailing establishment in question.

It is critical for us to decide on what our store should carry. At any given time, there are numerous alternatives. We must have a strong feel, and perhaps small data, for what would be appropriate and what would not. Sales volumes, the needs expressed by our target market and, once again, if possible, small data may be carefully analyzed before certain purchase decisions from the suppliers are made.

In managing product categories, stock keeping units (SKUs) must be carefully identified, because when combined they create meaningful categories.

In order to reiterate the importance of logistics, it is critical to state, once again, the entire logistics system needs to be integrated. While retail giants emphasize cost savings, by emphasizing out-of-store logistics, smaller independents may place more emphasis on in-store logistics first and combine both in-store and out-of-store logistics.

SUMMARY

Perhaps above all, this chapter identified some of the advantages of being independent. Certainly, the smaller independents must be managed by an entrepreneurial management. Such managements can adjust their activities to local conditions. Their product mixes, their advertising messages, being able to use local supply are only some of these freedoms. Certainly, the smaller independents cannot have the cost savings discounters could have, but they could be better in serving their customers. A critical area this chapter places some emphasis on is the in-store and out-of-store logistics being brought together and started by merchandise planning as part of in-store logistics.

15

STORE PERFORMANCE EVALUATION

It is extremely important that the retail store is evaluated regularly. Although it is important to evaluate the store's performance as a whole, it may be even more critical to determine which activities or sections of the store are doing well and which ones are needed to be evaluated carefully, because they may be performing, say, not up to par. Only if all of the activities are in a desirable form is it possible for the store to perform a synergistic overall performance. Careful evaluation of performance, in proper detail, also provides a learning curve of what to do and what not to do.

RETAILERS AS A LEARNING ORGANIZATION

Organizations, large or small, must learn continuously. However, learning takes two separate forms, proactive and reactive. A retailer, particularly a smaller independent one that does not have many resources to survive in the face of adversities in the marketplace, must be a proactive learner. This means that the retailer does not have much time to "just wait and see"; hence, reactive learning, even though it is taking place, is not sufficient. It is unfortunately easy for the smaller independent to become one of the about 650,000 companies disappearing yearly. The smaller independent must make a point of determining where the key decision areas regarding the functioning of the store are and how the market responds to these decisions.

Perhaps one of the most important points to be made here is that many smaller independents would consider research as a luxury item. Typically, they are in desperate need for information that would help them to learn how to cope with very dynamic and not necessarily friendly markets. A retail information management system (RIMS) is not a luxury, but a necessity for proactive learning. Here, careful information is gathered to help manage the store.

A learning retailer is proactive. Proactivity here implies systematic and careful scrutiny of the store's activities and the market's reactions.

Every store must have what are deemed early indicators carefully analyzed. Early reactions of the market to the store may provide valuable hints as to what is working and what is not as the retailer enters the market. For instance, the manager of a popular restaurant in a small southeastern town is used to seeing a reasonable line of people waiting to enter his restaurant for lunch every day about 11:30 a.m. One day as he arrives at the restaurant, he finds no one is waiting to enter. Certainly this is an indicator. But he cannot afford to wait and see what would happen. He has to find out what caused the early indicator. It could be a new more popular competitor, the new menu, the new group of servers, and some other possibilities.

What is important here is that first, the early indicator is noticed, second an immediate action is taken to determine the cause, and third an immediate decision to remedy the situation is made.

Of course, as the retailer reacts to early indicators and makes certain decisions and implements, then the subsequent reaction by the market is an important part of the learning process. As seen in Exhibit 15.1, reactions to store, that is, early indicators, lead to certain functional decisions. Those functional decisions have a certain impact on the market. If these can be effectively detected, then the plans for the overall retail functions can be constructed. Certainly, these plans are based on expected or desired reactions from the market. But the typical changes in the market may further force modification of these plans. These expected modifications raise the key question of "can we accomplish that?" Needless to say, the store's management is proactively learning from these sequences of events and activities.

Exhibit 15.1   A Retail Information Management System

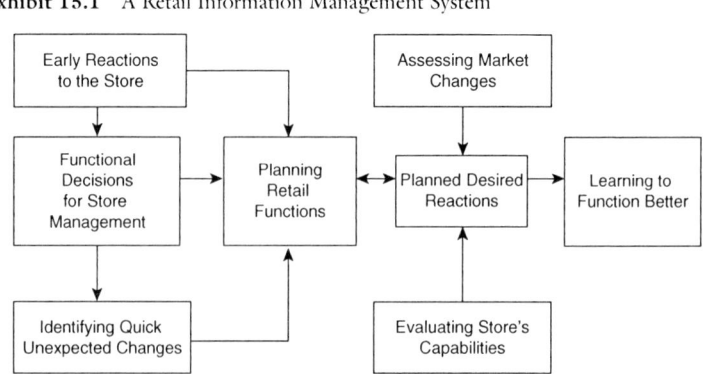

Source: Adapted and revised from Samli (2004).

A retail establishment located in the downtown of a major city in the Midwest has been a specialty leader for men's fashions. However, with the increased competition particularly from suburban shopping centers with some deterioration in the trading area, and significant changes in styles the store's profit picture became questionable. The reaction to early indicators of declining profit was to have a specialized line of products that would create differential congruence. It was decided that the store would carry a complete line of uniforms. The market reacted positively, and the profit picture became substantially more desirable.

The learning process led in the direction of planning the retail functions. As we learn more, these functions (such as the specifics of retail mixes) become more refined and more clearly defined. This is the value of being a learning organization and being proactive.

Certainly all the previous experiences of the store are crucial in regard to planning the desired results that the store aims to accomplish. Based on the specifics of the expected (or desired) results, the retail functions need to be planned. Here, understanding the changes in the market and their impact on our store is critical (Exhibit 15.1). Once the plans are implemented, we go back to early indicators. If necessary, the control function takes over and further revisions to the plans take place.

RETAIL MARKETING AUDITS

Although learning perpetually continues with proper control function, continuity in these relationships is materialized by attempting to develop formal marketing audits. Unfortunately, smaller independents' management, which is most likely to be the owner-manager, is typically so busy on day-to-day activities; developing a periodic audit system may not be in existence. Such an audit system must have two types of activities, internal and external.

Internal Retail Audits

Every retailer must be able to look at its practices candidly and critically. Such an orientation would also indicate the retailer's ability to learn and make its operations more successful. It is easy and extremely tempting to blame somebody or some force outside the store for the troubles it may have. This certainly is an escape mechanism that will do nothing to improve the current conditions. It does not lead to finding a solution to the problem that is being experienced. Just before the Christmas season, a few retailers in a southeast town decided that due to the national economic recession they should lower their costs. They cut down their advertising activity and they did not hire special help which they always did during that season. A study of the local consumers indicated that, they are not revising their plans of shopping during that season because of the national recession. The stores who cut down their costs did not do nearly as well as other retailers in the area.

Internal marketing audits for a retailer must revolve around at least ten key elements. Exhibit 15.2 emphasizes these elements. It must be noted that all of these lead to learning and improvement in performance. In small retailing some or all of these elements are ignored, again, since the management, or the owner-manager, is busy with routine day-to-day work. This is a major problem that needs to be remedied. Developing an internal retail audit must facilitate proactive plans for growth and competitiveness and, above all, learning from the process.

Of all ten points of emphasis, the first one is the most critical and most problematic. If the store management cannot evaluate itself and its capabilities, it will never be able to conduct an objective and constructive internal audit.

But, performing an objective self-evaluation is a very difficult assignment. It may require an outside help, perhaps, in the form of consulting. It must be stated forcefully that it is a must.

All of the other factors listed in Exhibit 15.2 have been discussed in different chapters of this book. It is difficult to prioritize these variables; some of them are more important under special circumstances. The retail management must be in a position to identify those.

Exhibit 15.2   The Key Elements of a Retail Internal Audit

- Store Management's Self-Evaluation
- Store Customer Relations
- Store Personnel Management and Customer Service
- Store's Merchandise Mix and Inventory Control
- Store's Budget Controls and Spending
- Store's Ability to Buy, Its Credit and Finances
- Store's Pricing Policies and Strategy
- Store's Displays, Layout, and Ambience
- Store's Advertising and Sales Promotion
- Store's Ability to use Social Media
- Store's Plans for Growth

External Audits

Understanding the existing conditions under which the retail establishment is functioning is important for all retailers. However, it is reasonable to make a case for internal audits being more important for smaller independents. External audits, on the other hand, are much more critical for large retailers' performance, which may be closely tied to the existing conditions in their markets and trading areas. Additionally, large retailers are under pressure to compete with their equally large (or larger) competitors. This creates a special need for external audits examining the retailer's competitiveness considering economic conditions and competitive forces.

Exhibit 15.3 illustrates the key elements of an external audit. Although some of these elements also are dealt with in different chapters, they are briefly discussed below.

The status of the national economy. When the national economy sneezes, the retailing sector, particularly large retailers, catches pneumonia. Some fallout may also reach small retailers as well. For instance, when the national economy was doing well during the late 1990s the limited, for instance, did quite well, similarly in a following recessionary period, consumers may opt for classical and more durable casual clothing. During that period Gap, which is the chain with more classical clothing, performed much better than The Limited, which is the chain that has been more flashy and fashionable.

The conditions in the store's trading area. A major construction activity that may divert the vehicular traffic drastically and block access to retailing facilities can be significantly critical for local smaller independents. In some extreme cases, these retailers simply cannot survive.

Critical changes in immediate competition. In much of rural America, in small towns a phenomenon has been very noticeable during the past

Exhibit 15.3   The Key Elements of a Retail External Audit

- The Status of the National Economy
- The Conditions of the Store's Trading Area
- Critical Changes in Immediate Competition
- Executed Changes in the Competitive Picture
- Any Unexpected Changes in the Store's Image
- New Profit Opportunities to be Pursued
- Changing Expectations of Consumers
- Emergence of New Suppliers

four decades or so, that is, Walmart. In many cases, a Walmart unit located out of town has created disaster for the town's retailing. The only thing the local retailers can do, in such cases, as has been pointed out throughout this book, is improving their services and personalizing their customers. This calls for joint effort by local retailers that has not been the tradition.

Expected changes in the competitive picture. If, for instance, Small Town A expects a major retailing complex to be built in Larger Town B next door, there may be many changes in the existing local competitive picture. Similarly, if, for instance, the major mall in town is bought by an outside investment company and the total profile of the small mall is going to be changed and rumor has it many imported products are to be sold there, these changes may make local retailers think carefully and react constructively.

Any unexpected changes in store image. A small independent pizzeria in a small southeastern university town encountered a rumor that one of its chefs had hepatitis. Without being able to resort to any kind of defense, the pizzeria went out of business. Any kind of deterioration in the store image could easily create similar situations.

New profit opportunities to be pursued. When aerobics suddenly became very popular in the 1980s, many sporting goods stores immediately reacted by making aerobics attire and supplies available. Similarly, the emergence of healthy yogurt with many various flavors, say, Chobani yogurt, created a very successful image. Such developments could create many new opportunities in retailing.

Changing expectations of consumers. As middle-class America shrank, typical middle-class consumers that happened to be Sears customers changed their expectations and moved down slightly to Target or further down to Walmart. Sears responded by imitating Walmart and offering "everyday low prices" but that strategy simply did not appeal to its customers, since they could go to Target or Walmart; Sears' approach was not attractive. Changing expectations of consumers, particularly the store customers, can be a major shock to the retailer, particularly if that is not expected.

Emergence of new supplies. About four decades ago there were not as many "competent suppliers" in the world of providing a large variety of products to be sold to consumers everywhere. The so-called four tigers of Asia, that is, Hong Kong, South Korea, Taiwan, and Singapore, all emerged during that time and became powerful participants in world trade. When the flattening of the world (Friedman 2005) came about, more small-scale suppliers entered the world trade with many new products as well as parts of finished products. Now China itself has become a discount player. American retailers, particularly small independents, are entering the international arena and buying discounted products to be offered to their target markets. It must be noted that elements of both internal and external audits have various meanings and varying importance for different retailers. Therefore, each retailer may perhaps wish to evaluate these audits according to their needs from very critical to not very important.

OTHER CONTROL ACTIVITY

It has already been mentioned that inventory controls are critical. With modern information technology, it is possible for large and small retailers to develop a perpetual inventory control mechanism. Such mechanisms are more practical and perhaps necessary for smaller independents, since large retailers have major hindrances to maintaining inventory data integrity. Such hindrances may emerge from selling errors, receiving errors, merchandise stocking errors, database errors, and physical inventory counting errors. However, without a good database, inventory controls are impossible, and a store cannot possibly maintain competitiveness without a good inventory control practice. In recent years such data are used for different control calculations. Among these are gross margin return on inventory (GMROI), dollar contribution return on inventory (DCROI), and gross margin return on merchandise investment (GMROMI) (Berman and Evans 2013; Levy and Weitz 2012). Such technical analysis could provide valuable information to further set the course of the retail establishment, both large and small (Samli 2004). One final thing must be kept in mind that control mechanisms lead to corrective action, and since retailing takes place in constantly changing markets, continuous control activity must be considered a necessity.

SUMMARY

This chapter makes a critical statement regarding retail establishments to become learning organizations. Systematic audits are part of this learning process. Similarly, audits facilitate control activity meaning that the retail establishment is on its course of desired plans of performance. Two types of audits are identified in this chapter, internal and external. While the external audits may be very important for retailing giants, internal audits are critical for smaller independents. These audits provide the foundation for evaluating the store's performance to reach its goals and succeed.

Finally, it is maintained that the control process must be continuous. Since retailing is a very dynamic undertaking occurring in an ever-changing market system, the continuity of the control function can provide corrective action and improvement in retail activities.

POSTSCRIPT

A brief postscript is important here to pull the whole set of ideas and experiences together and to provide a bird's-eye view for the reader.

- First and above all, 650,000 small business disappears yearly, of which most are small retailers, is a very costly proposition to our society. If the practices are followed as discussed in this book this number may go down substantially. This certainly is my hope.
- Whereas large-scale retailers are very sensitive to national economic trends and must carefully analyze what their competitors are doing, smaller independents are more concerned about local trends and consumer sentiments. They are geared more toward catering to their well-defined target markets or niches than worrying what the national trends are.
- As national retail giants try to offer more standardized and discounted products, smaller independents concentrate on more localized and specialized merchandise. If possible, this is one way they can distinguish themselves from national discounting giants.
- Smaller independents provide a more personalized atmosphere in their stores. Discounting giants mostly do not bother with, that gives the smaller independents opportunity to develop relationship marketing which is aimed at long-term mutual understanding with their regular customers.
- This book is written primarily for smaller independents in retailing. It mainly says, "if you cannot be cheaper you could be better and here is how".
- Most cost-driven national retail giants offer a physical atmosphere of not distinction. Smaller independents can do much better.
- National discounting giants treat their customers as computerized members, whereas the smaller independents could treat their customers as persons and important human beings.
- If the smaller independents want to survive and succeed, they must become learning organizations. They must learn what works and what does not work at the local level and must always be in tune with the sentiments of their customers.

- Smaller independents create jobs and generate innovations that will make the local economies and their target market customers happy. Local political authorities must be very cognizant of this aspect of entrepreneurial retailing.
- Owner-managers of smaller independents deal not only with economic and managerial issues but also with psychological issues pertaining to their customers. Hence, they have to be multitalented in order to generate consumer value and improve prevailing quality of life.

In discussing management of the retail establishment, time and again, the differential congruence principle has been discussed throughout this book. The retail establishment can do well by differentiating itself on the basis of target market preferences. Such congruence creates store loyalty, which is absolutely critical for the retailer. Because they are more versatile and flexible than the discounting giants, smaller independents can be very successful if they can achieve differential congruence.

Finally, implied throughout the book but not articulated adequately is that market research is essential. If that can be combined with small data, the smaller independents could definitely gain an edge over discounting giants and make a major contribution to the economic wellbeing of the country.

REFERENCES

Anonymous (2014). "Retailers Use Social to Spur Shopping," E-Marketer, February.

Berman, Barry and Evans, Joel R. (2012). *Retail Management*. Upper Saddle River, NJ: Prentice Hall.

Berman, Barry and Evans, Joel (2013). *Retail Giants*. Mason, OH: Thomson.

Berman, Jillian (2014). "Clear Evidence That Costco and the Wal-Mart Lived in Totally Different Worlds." *Huffington Post*, May 29.

Biesdorf, Stefan, Court, David, and Wilmott, Paul (2013). "Big Data: What Is Your Plan?" *McKinsey Quarterly* 2: 8.

Boyle, Mathew (2003). "Brand Killers." *Fortune* August: 89–100.

Brown, Brad, Chui, Michael, and Manyika, James (2012). "Are You Ready for the Era of Big Data?" *Inter Media* May: 28–33.

Conor, Flynn (2014). "From Clicks to Bricks," Kimco Blog, Jan 2, 2014.

Derickson, L. (2013). "Effectiveness of Small Business Technology Tools." *E-Strategy Trends*, March 15.

Desrochers, Debra M., Gundlach, Gregory T., and Foer, Albert A. (2003). "Analysis of Antitrust Challenges to Category Captain Arrangements." *Journal of Public Policy and Marketing* Fall: 1–16.

Executive Summary (1999). www.cpfr.org, December 9.

Festinger, Leon (1957). *A Theory of Cognitive Dissonance*. Stanford: Stanford University Press.

Fisbein, Martin (1967). "A Behavior Theory Approach to the Relations Between Beliefs about an Object and the Attitude towards That Object," in *Readings in Attitude Theory and Measurement*. New York: John Wiley and Sons.

Flikinger, Burt P. III (1995). "Wal-Mart vs. the World: Who Wins?" *Progressive Grocer*, April 19.

Friedman, Thomas L. (2005). *The World Is Flat*. New York: Farrar, Straus and Giroux.

Hirschman, Elizabeth C. (1979). "Retail Competitive Structure: Present and Potential," in *Educators Conference Proceedings*, ed. Neil Beckwith et al. Chicago, IL: American Marketing Association.

Hulten, Bertil, Broweus, Niklas, and Van Dijk, Marcus (2009). *Sensory Marketing*. New York: Palgrave Macmillan.

Leah, Rikard (1995). "Supercenters Entice Shoppers," Advertising Age, March 1–10.

Levy, Michael and Weitz, Barton A. (2012). *Retailing Management*. New York: McGraw Hill Irwin.

Maslow, A. H. (1964). "A Theory of Human Motivation," in *Readings in Managerial Psychology*, ed. H. I. Levi and L. R. Pond. Chicago, IL: University of Chicago Press.

McAfee, Andrew and Brynjolfson, Erik (2013). "Big Data." *Harvard Business Review* Oct: 59–68.

Naisbitt, J. (1982). *Megatrends.* New York: Warner Books.

Peters, Tom (1989). *Thriving on Chaos.* New York: Alfred A. Knopf.

Progressive Grocer (1995). "Toward a Revised Theory of Category Management," August, 36.

Raghavendra, Kamath (2014). "Retailers Seem to Prefer Stand-Alone Stores to Malls," Interim Budget, 17 Feb.

Samli, A. Coskun (1996). *Information-Driven Marketing Decisions.* Westport, CT: Quorum Books.

Samli, A. Coskun (1998). *Retail Marketing Strategy Westport*, Quorum Book.

Samli, A. Coskun (2004). *Up against the Retail Giants.* Mason, OH: Thomson.

Samli, A. Coskun (2012). *International Consumer Behavior in the 21st Century.* New York: Springer.

Samli, A. Coskun (2013). *From Market Economy to a Finance Economy.* New York: Palgrave Macmillan.

Samli, A. C. and Choi, Y. T. (2014). "High Touch Component of Modern Retailing," an unpublished study.

Samli, A. Coskun and Gupta, Saurabh (2014). "Utilization of Small Data for Smaller Size Retailing: Gaining an Edge over Discount Giants," paper in progress.

Samli, A. Coskun and Ongan N. Mehmet (1996). "Retail Human Resource Management: An Exploration and Research Agenda." *Journal of Marketing Channels*, September: 81–99.

Samli, A. Coskun and Shaw, Eric (2002). "Achieving Managerial Synergism: Balancing Strategic Business Units and Profit Centers." *Journal of Market Focused Management* Fall: 59–75.

SBA (2012). "Frequently Asked Questions," www.sba.gov/advocacy.

Schlesinger, Leonard A. and Hesket, James L. (1991). "Enhancement of Service Workers." *California Management Review* Summer: 83–99.

Silverstein, Michael J. and Fiske, Neil (2005). *Trading Up.* New York: Portfolio.

Strauss, Judy, El-Ansary, Adel., and Frost, Raymond (2006). *E-Marketing.* Upper Saddle River, NJ: Prentice Hall.

Supermarket Guru (2003). Quick Poll Results, July 11, 1–3.

Ton, Zeynep (2014). *Good Jobs Strategy.* MIT Sloan School of Management.

Wilkie, William L. (1994). *Consumer Behavior.* New York: John Wiley and Sons.

ABOUT THE AUTHOR

Dr. A. Coskun (Josh) Samli is Research Professor of Marketing and International Business at the University of North Florida.

Dr. Samli received his bachelor's degree from Istanbul Academy of Commercial Sciences (currently Marmara University), his MBA from the University of Detroit, and his PhD from Michigan State University. As a Ford Foundation Fellow, he has done postdoctoral work at UCLA, the University of Chicago, and as an International Business Program Fellow at New York University.

In 1974–1975, he was a Sears-AACSB Federal Faculty Fellow in the Office of Policy and Plans, US Maritime Administration. In 1983, Dr. Samli was invited to New Zealand as the Erskine Distinguished Visiting Scholar to lecture and undertake research at Canterbury University. In 1985, Dr. Samli was a Fulbright Distinguished Lecturer in Turkey. He was selected as the Beta Gamma Sigma, L. J. Buchan Distinguished Professor for the academic year 1986–1987 to work at North Carolina Agricultural and Technical University. He was given a research fellowship by the Center of Science Development, South Africa, February 1995. He was awarded a fellowship by the Finnish Academy of Sciences to teach a doctoral seminar in June 1999.

Dr. Samli is the author or coauthor of more than 250 scholarly articles, 21 books, and 30 monographs. Dr. Samli has been invited as a distinguished scholar to deliver papers in many parts of the world by many universities. He has lectured extensively in Europe, Eastern Europe, the Middle East, the Far East, Oceania, and many other parts of the world. He was very active in the Fulbright Commission. Dr. Samli is on the review board of seven major journals. He was the first president and a research fellow of the International Society for Quality of Life Studies (ISQOLS).

Dr. Samli is a Distinguished Fellow in the Academy of Marketing Science and a past chairman of its board of governors. He has done some of the earlier studies on the poor, elderly, and price discrimination. Dr. Samli is a research fellow of International Society for Quality of Life Studies. He is cofounder and was the first president of this organization. His most recent books are: *Entering and Succeeding in Third World Countries*, Thomson (2004); *Up against the Retail Giants*, Thomson (2005); *Chaotic Markets*, Praeger (2007); and *Globalization from the Bottom Up*, Springer (2008); and *International Entrepreneurship*, Springer (2009). Two earlier books—*Social Responsibility in Marketing* (1993) and *Empowering the American Consumer* (2001)—were considered among the most important academic books in the United States by *Choice Magazine*, which managed by librarians.

Dr. Samli has worked with hundreds of small and medium-sized businesses as a consultant over a 50-year period and he has conducted many seminars before hundreds of business managers and graduate students in Turkey.

Dr. Samli has had more than 25,000 students from all over the world. Many of them are professors, successful businessmen, and statesmen. He reviews dissertations as an outside international expert. Dr. Samli was recipient of Harold Berkman Service to the Discipline Award given by the Academy of Marketing Science in 2008. During the summers of 2008 and 2009 he was the recipient of the Evren Professorship at Florida Atlantic University.

In 2010 he was awarded the first James M. Parrish Faculty Award at University of North Florida.

INDEX

Lightning Source UK Ltd.
Milton Keynes UK
UKOW05n0013240415

250206UK00004B/46/P